A Home To Call My Own

A German World War II Refugee's Story of God's Providence

Willi G. Schakat

A Home To Call My Own
A German World War II Refugee's Story of God's Providence
by Willi G. Schakat

Printed in the United States of America

ISBN 9781498409520

www.xulonpress.com

Dedication

I want to dedicate this book to my wife Judith, who early on suggested that I write my story for posterity's sake. For a long time I didn't begin the project, but in the late 1980s my children asked many questions about my life story, so I finally decided to get going. It was Judith who encouraged me along the way. Judith loved history, and somehow my life's story was fascinating to her. In the meantime, our children grew up, but they still asked me questions about my life. Today, our three sons, Timothy, Thomas, and William, share dad's life story along with Judith. My boys worked hard to get this project together. They spent hours sorting through my grammar issues. My sentence structure is influenced by German even though I've been in America for fifty-eight years. Needless to say they had a difficult task to present my thoughts clearly. Most of all, they never let me quit. Judith, however, was never able to see the final draft since her untimely death in 2005. But her heart's desire to leave my life's story to her children and grandchildren is finally complete.

Acknowledgments

*S*ometimes God brings people into our lives that have a dramatic impact on us. I had several people who impacted the course of my life that I want to acknowledge. The first was my Aunt Ottilie, my mother's sister. After the war, she wondered what had happened to her sister's children. She knew her sister had died, but whatever became of the children? She searched through various agencies and any connection in Germany she could remember. She did not cease to search! When she finally found out that our family had resettled in West Germany, she came and sought us out. A year later she became the sponsor of my sister Gerda and me to come to America. We got our visas and in December of 1956 we arrived in America. But even more than that, she was a woman of faith. She planted the seed in my future faith. She died one month shy of her 106th birthday!

The second was my Aunt Irene, by marriage. She married my mother's brother. She too told me all about my mother, since I was three-and-one-half years old when she died. Hardship in her younger life made her a determined person. She spent eight years in

Siberia, Russia, in a labor camp after the Russians secured the territory that had been occupied by Germans. She also had a great love for the Lord. I spent many hours with Aunt Irene as she told me things about my mother, particularly things she endured through her illness. She told me how my mother laughed, cried, and cared for us when we were little. Aunt Irene also lived to be 105 and I so appreciated her.

There is yet another person that played a role in my youth: Maria Lange. I call her "Aunt," but she is of no blood relative to me. My mother and Maria were playmates in their youth. I will mention Maria in my story. I met Maria, not in Europe, but in a post office in Cincinnati, Ohio, a few days after my arrival in America. As we talked in the post office that day, and she heard my name, *Schakat,* she said she knew my mother! She told me about the things they played as girls, and Maria was even at my parent's wedding! I had always longed to hear stories about my mother, and here, in Ohio, I met one of my mother's closest friends! Maria and her family were instrumental in bringing my maternal grandma out of Lithuania. Maria also lived to be around ninety years old.

So these three ladies played a major role in my life, but most importantly, they were spiritual giants, and they made an everlasting impact. I will always cherish the memories I have of them, and I look forward to our reunion in heaven.

A Home to Call My Own:
A German World War II Refugee's Story of God's Providence
Willi G. Schakat

Author's Preface

*H*ave you ever wondered about the so-called accidents in life? I have. How often have difficulties occurred on the road to maturity? God seems sometimes so far away and the next time so very near. Then it seems He has wonderful ways of turning what seem to be some "accidents" or "detours" into answers that shape our lives. The Apostle Paul testified in Philippians 1:12 that even his imprisonment turned out to be good for the furtherance of the gospel. Like me, I'm sure most of you have discovered that some of the greatest opportunities in our lives occurred when everything went wrong (at least in our own thinking). The "detours" or trials of my life started when I was about six years of age. These are the events that God ordained to make me into the man I am today. I remember many of the things that happened to me all these years later. So the story of my life seemed to start out one way, but God changed the course.

Isaiah 55:8-9 reads, "For My thoughts are not your thoughts, neither are your ways my ways, declares the Lord. For as the heavens are higher than the earth, so are my ways higher than your ways, and my thoughts higher than your thoughts." Dear reader, as you read my story, please be aware of God leading any of us throughout our lives even though we are not consciously aware of it. I certainly was not conscious of His leading. But we must reckon that a greater power than we is at work in the world whether we believe it or not. Some of us have gone through life without any trouble or hardship whatsoever, but reading my story I wonder now how I have ever made it, other than a higher power at work in my life. Whether it was survival under extreme hardships, or protection when all hope was gone, or guidance as a young man when there was no way out, I just cannot imagine that all happened by chance. As early as twenty years of age, I wondered, "How did I ever make it?" If we are honest with ourselves, we probably ask the same question. It was God in His gracious providence that kept me in His care. Psalm 115:3 says, "Our God is in the heavens; he does all that he pleases." The difference between fate and providence is that fate has no meaning. According to fate, there is no source driving any event, and therefore, all things really are meaningless. However, providence speaks of purpose, that is, God's purposes. God is working all things for the glory of his name. God is sovereign over all events in your life and in mine. He is working his purposes in spite of the effects sin has had in our world. The rise of Hitler and the Nazi regime could not prevent God from calling out a people for himself. God graciously saved me, not from a wicked ruler, or out of tragic circumstances, but He saved me from my sin and from the coming judgment of God. I am here by God's grace alone. He worked my life in such a way that I would come to know him and submit to him as King. As you read this story, look for the hand of God. Read and see if it isn't true in your life, too.

Willi G. Schakat

Introduction

We three sons have gone through our lives hearing all kinds of pronunciations of our last name. It is not every day that one in America comes across the name of *Schakat*. It is actually quite comical to hear the different variations. This often leads to the question of its origin. Our name has provided us many opportunities to share some of the unique experiences of our father, who was a refugee during WWII. Our father's story really is one of sovereign grace and mercy. Literally millions were killed in Europe during this time. Stalin killed millions, not only Germans and Poles, but also his own people in Russia. Of course Hitler ordered the execution of millions of Jews. He also euthanized many of the elderly and those born with birth defects. Political opponents and clergymen were also killed. Death was all over Europe. The chances of survival were grim for refugees too. The only explanation of why our dad is alive today is this: God had so willed to spare him, to lead him to America, and most importantly, to save him from the wrath of God and to promise him *A Home to Call His Own*.

We are proud to be the sons of this German immigrant to America. He gave us a childhood that was so much better than his own. He taught us the value of a dollar and the virtue of hard work. He always has a smile on his face, and he has never met a stranger. Most of all, he pointed us to Jesus Christ, our only hope in this life and the life to come. As believers in Jesus Christ, we hope these pages do the same for you, for we recognize that the best way to honor our dad is to lead others to this hope. We also are refugees, aliens, and strangers in a world to which we do not belong. "Our citizenship is in heaven, and from it we await a Savior, the Lord Jesus Christ" (Philippians 3:20). There He has prepared a home for those He has called.

One of my sons Bill's favorite modern hymns is one we sing at church called "It's Been Mercy All the Way," by John G. Elliott. Read the words of this song and then our dad's story. Think of all your goings and comings (Psalm 121:8). I believe we all can say that God has kept us by His mercy alone.

Lord I thank you for your faithful mercy,

All my footsteps have been guarded by grace.

From this moment on my heart will praise you.

Lord I love you, Lord I love you.

Refrain:

Mercy, mercy, goodness and kindness, love and forgiveness.

Mercy, mercy, it's been mercy all the way.

You have loved me with a great compassion

You have spared me from the pain I deserved.

Here's my heart O may it bring you pleasure,

Lord I love you, Lord I love you.

Tim, Tom, and Bill Schakat

April 22, 2014

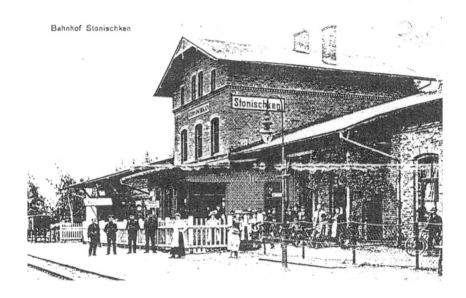

Bahnhof Stonischken

Chapter 1

From Birth to Flight

Day by day and with each passing moment,
strength I find to meet my trials here;
Trusting in my father's wise bestowment,
I've no cause for worry or for fear.
He whose heart is kind beyond all measure gives
unto each day what he deems best.
Lovingly, its part of pain and pleasure,
mingling toil with peace and rest.

Carolina Sandell Berg, 1865

I was born in a little village called Stonischken, East Prussia, on April 16, 1937, an area called in German the *Memelland*. It was a quaint little town. I never knew the exact population, but someone told me that there were about 300 residents at the time. The town had a grocery store, a post office, and a mill of some sort. I do not recall whether it was a lumber mill or a grain mill, but there were always trains coming in and out of this little town. Stonischken was a strategic place for the German Army because of the train station. German trains often stopped there on their way to the eastern front, carrying supplies for the war. Almost daily trains stopped here for the war effort. As young boys we curiously hopped on the train to see the engine and things. They usually came at night so that no one would see them. The Allied airplanes (those primarily were English, American and Russian planes) flew over almost every night to spy out the German movements.

The Memel River was the eastern-most border of Germany. The *Memelland* lay beyond the border that Germany had annexed sometime around 1938 or 1939. Historically, it was more in German possession than in Lithuanian. I remember on the Kurische Nehrung, an island on the Baltic Sea, there was a cemetery that had crosses and inscriptions in German dating from the eleventh century. It was a beautiful area with lots of unending fields, rich soil, and good harvests of all kinds of grains and potatoes and fruits and vegetables. It had wonderful lakes and dark forests, with birch trees lining all the roads. Sandy beaches were on the Baltic, and dark soil was everywhere. Farmers had lots of black and white cows, and horses were almost exclusively used for transportation. Even the state of East Prussia is and was called the, "Land der dunkelen Waelder und Cristalian Seas" (translated, "Land of dark forests and crystal seas"). It was the breadbasket of Germany. Its cities were clean and rich with historical monuments. The Baltic Sea was the gateway to foreign lands.

Our little village Stonischken was on the supply route for the German Army. I remember all the trains headed east to the warfront that came right past the train station where we lived. My parents had leased the railroad restaurant there, so we were a little familiar with what was going on. Although as a six year old I had little comprehension of what was going on in the war, I was intrigued by the locomotives that had the inscription on them, "Rader mussen rollen fur den Sieg" ("Wheels have to roll for the Victory"). I lived in Stonischken until I was six years old.

Little do I remember from my youth in Stonischken. However, a couple of things come to my remembrance. Like all little boys I loved candy. My family had owned, rented, or leased a restaurant there (I don't know for sure which), where we sold, besides food and drink, sweets—chocolate and candy. I remember that I would sneak behind the counter, grab some candy, and run behind the large wood stove in the corner of the waiting room to eat it there. Sometimes my sisters helped me. Some of the candy had sweet filling in it, and that was always the best.

Another incident I remember was when I was about four years old. I went to our little outhouse. The outhouse was about fifty meters from the house. I know I very seldom closed the door when I used it. One day sitting happily "on the throne," I saw a field mouse right ahead of me. I left my clothes lying on the floor and ran after the mouse and even caught it. Never minding to go back and get my clothes, I took the mouse and brought it close to the house where some utility poles were lying. I held the mouse by the tail and let it run to the end of the pole. Then I dragged it back to repeat the whole thing a couple of times. Finally one patron waiting in the station knocked on the window and pointed at me. I noticed then that I didn't have my clothes on. So I let the mouse go and ran to the outhouse to retrieve my underwear!

Like all little boys I liked to visit my grandma. Our grandpa had died many years before. She lived in a little village called *Pageldienen*. It was three or four kilometers from our house. My father was also born there. In the summer, my Aunt Marta took me there on the back seat of her bike. In the winter we went by a horse-drawn sled. We would run through the fields and play hide-and-seek-and find all kinds of entertainment. The fine sand was always our favorite. We liked to go barefoot but grandma forbade us on

Sundays. Only when the pastor's children were allowed to go barefoot could we then do the same. She was funny about that! The winters were extremely cold. Many times the well was frozen solid. I remember grandma would get bucket after bucket of snow to melt for our drinking water and cooking. On really cold nights she would let me sleep on top of the stove. Now the stove was not like one that we know. It was at least ten feet by ten feet, fired with wood or peat moss, and always on and warmed the kitchen area. There was another stove in the eating-living room area. This one was big enough to stand against for warmth. It also had a box where things could be warmed. Grandma would put our clothes in it before we got up in the morning to warm them up. I just loved being at grandma's house. She had this certain love and concern for the grandchildren that made us always to want to be there.

We also had some help in the restaurant. Father was drafted into the German Army, but before he left he hired a young girl to help with the work. Her name was Marta. My sister told me that she was mature for her fifteen years of age, and we needed her help since my mother was already sick and mostly in the hospital

At some time my sister Lilli was sent to an Erholungskur in Silesia (a former German province now in Poland). It was something like a rest and relaxation haven, because as a child, she was a little sickly and needed a place to recoup. When she came home one day, we were watching for the express train to go by, but it did not stop at Stonischken. It went to Heidekrug a little further away, and then returned with a local train back to Stonischken. Well, we saw Lilli wave at us from the speeding train. My sister Gerda was there along with a man named Mr. Plickert, the rail road officer, who held me up on that picket fence. I still have a picture from that occasion.

Shortly after my sixth birthday I did start school. I think it was only a short time that I went there because rumor had it that we might have to leave our home because of the war. The school was in a little town called Rucken, about three kilometers from Stonischken. The first day, my Aunt Marta took me on the backseat of her bicycle. But from then on we walked every day. There were a couple of lessons I did learn there. The school teacher made us show every morning that we had a handkerchief and clean fingernails. One morning I forgot my handkerchief, and the teacher made me go in front of the class and explain how I would blow my nose if I don't carry a handkerchief. I remember standing before the class and saying in a slow tone of voice, "Ich zieh den Snudder hoch" (I suck the snot up.) Everybody laughed, but I just stood there and wondered what the commotion was all about. This is naturally not a nice thing to say, but it did happen, and I remember it to this day. It also was a great teaching method that one never forgot. Not only were we required to have a handkerchief and clean fingernails, but also a small pocketknife and a short piece of string. That was for emergencies in case something needed to be repaired. Even first graders had to learn to be ready for anything. The reason for the clean fingernail was because most of us lived in the country, and grooming was not a priority with most of us. (In the summer 1999 I had the privilege to return for a visit to my homeland and to reminisce of some of my youthful experiences. I also visited the school at Rucken, and the incident came right back to me.)

My mother died when I was just three-and-one-half years old in February 1941. I have hardly any recollection of her for some reason. Mother became very sick and spent the last two years of her life mostly in the hospital. That's probably the reason that I have absolutely no recollection of her. She died of cancer, I was told. I remember the funeral very well, however. My father fought in the war in Russia and had come home for the funeral. He brought me a pair of Russian felt boots and chocolate. The boots, I remember,

had no hard soles on them, because in Russia the ground is so frozen
that it makes no difference whether one has soles or not. They were,
however, very warm. I remember the day of the funeral father held
me on his arms and gave me flowers to throw into the grave. This
would be the last time in 1941 that I would see my father until a few
days after Christmas 1946.

Chapter 2

Running for Our Lives

A Mighty Fortress is our God; A bulwark never failing. Our Helper He amid the flood; of mortal ills prevailing. For still our ancient foe, dost seek to work us woe. His craft and power are great, and armed with cruel hate. On earth is not his equal.

Martin Luther, 1529

*T*he war got worse. Daily we observed air raids. The next largest city, called Tilsit, was heavily bombed. I remember one night that a train full of ammunition left our station and headed for Tilsit. That train was hit as it entered the Tilsit train station and went up in smoke in the air. Railroad stations were the first targets of bombing. We would watch the bombs fall every night from eighteen kilometers away. Our station had a bomb shelter where we hid almost every night. Refugees started to head west. Since we were a little connected to the German railroad, the authorities of the railroad provided us with a freight car, and we packed most of our belongings and took the last train out, heading to West Prussia, to the City of Mohrungen in the beginning of August 1944. Before we left, I remember Tante Marta came and told us, "Draussen alle Kuehe weinen." That is translated, "Outside all the cows are crying." Here is what happened: before all the farmers left their houses and fled, they let all the cows from the barns and pastures loose, and the cows were full of milk, which was extremely painful to them, and the cows let out this peculiar cry. This is a sight I trust I will never experience again.

The intensity of the war grew even worse, and refugees were everywhere. Having arrived in Mohrungen by train, we stayed in a house on the second floor. I remember we had to go up on an outside stairwell to our second floor apartment. There are just a few things I remember of our stay there. I remember Tante Marta made potato pancakes there for the children. We all helped her peel the potatoes in an old wash pan. It was here that German Army units arrived from the front, and soon there was street fighting going on all over town. We stayed in Mohrungen altogether less than five months.

Pommeria, another province of Germany, now Poland, was our next destination. The Russian army made rapid advances. We stayed with a farm family. Only the wife and children remained.

It was in this little town, called Linde, Kreis or (County) Greifenhagen where the Russians overtook us. For three days, every morning they drove with tanks through the town and looked for the next victim. At first they hunted the mayor, and then the postmaster. Many young girls were raped in the morning and shut in at night. Since we were strangers there also, the locals came at night to the farm where we stayed and decided to flee the next night. We all were afraid. We heard some folks say that it was better to commit suicide than fall into the hands of the enemy. But at last it was decided to attempt to flee. So at 11 pm that night, we put on all the clothes we could put on, made some sandwiches, and took off, leaving everything we owned behind. We ran into the forest. We saw some searchlights from the enemy army, but they never did see us. The Russian soldiers were usually drunk at night. It was "every man for himself" for us; no one could help the other. I was almost seven-and-one-half years old. We crossed a very muddy field but kept on going. I was close to my sisters and followed the townspeople into the forest. We had gone about forty minutes into the forest when we realized that my Tante Marta and my grandmother were no longer with us. We mentioned that to the people, and they just told us, "You are on your own" and left us. We three—my sisters Lilli, Gerda and I—went back the best we knew how. As we approached the edge of the forest and saw the hilly fields, we recognized in the twilight three soldiers and my Tante Marta and grandmother. We knew at this point that this was perhaps our last moment on earth. We approached them, and to our surprise, these were German soldiers fleeing in the night themselves. We also were happy to see our aunt and grandmother. But our reunion and joy were short lived when grandmother told us that she had lost both of her shoes when she crossed that muddy field and could no longer go with us. Since time was of the essence now, we kissed grandmother good-bye, never to see her again. Our aunt too, had to make a big decision: either to go with her mother or to continue with her brother's children. She chose to go with us. (My Tante Marta was buried in Berlin in January of 2000.) She was a remarkable woman. She did everything possible to raise us. She never got married until we were reunited with our father. Having left grandmother with heavy hearts, we continued, all four of us, along with the soldiers. (This was the last time we saw our grandmother alive, although we heard years later that she made it back to our home village.)

That night we walked about forty kilometers (25 mi.). We walked through empty villages and over bombed out bridges. It was just an eerie feeling. The next morning we encountered a farm family still in their home. We told them where we came from and convinced them to leave. He had a tractor with an open trailer and some fuel. I remember that it was freezing cold. We all boarded the trailer and for the next two days drove as far as we could. My recollection was that we ran out of fuel. However, we drove over frozen rivers, including the Oder River, which is now the border between Germany and Poland. It was so cold that one child froze to death. I remember how some women nursed children just to warm them and to keep them from crying, even though they had nothing to give them.

Chapter 3

Death, Destruction, and Denmark

Every day the Lord himself is near me with a special
mercy for each hour;
All my cares he fain would bear and cheer me, he
whose name is Counselor and Power.
The protection of his child and treasure is a charge
that on himself has laid;
"As your days, your strength shall be in measure,"
this the pledge to me he made.

Carolina Sandell Berg, 1865

Even though I walk through the valley of the shadow
of death, I will fear no evil, for you are with me. Your
rod and your staff, they comfort me. Psalm 23:4.

*T*he next two months, according to my recollection, were just
terrible. The winter of 1944–45 was the coldest in memory.
For months the temperature was below freezing, and the snow was
so deep that it came up to the belly of horses and cows. Some people
used cows for their wagons because they provided some milk for
nourishment, but even that failed in the end since animal feed ran

out or the animals starved or froze to death. Not thousands but millions of East Prussian Germans fled the advancing Russian Army. It is said that the population of East Prussia was at the time about 2.5 million people, but during those crucial months, every fourth person, about 600,000, died in that below-freezing weather. The toll of human suffering, the death of women, children, and animals was just horrible. As a young child, I could not fathom the suffering. Even today, I cannot fathom the amount of total loss of precious human beings. I heard of a nine-year-old girl say to her father, "Vater, erschiess mich," which, translated, means, "Father, shoot me." On every side of the road, in the surrounding fields, in trenches, in empty villages, lay bodies of mostly women and children, frozen to death. Some were so weak that they could not go on any more. Those that were alive wished for rapid death rather than having to go further. My recollections as a seven-year-old are somewhat vague as far as some details of those months of fleeing, but I remember some adult conversations that became the talk during those many days. For hundreds of thousands of refugees, the trek to the West became a type of inferno for most. People just either froze to death, became so sick that they couldn't go any longer, were shot to death by the Russian army, or were raped. That was the most feared practice that women had to endure. The cruelty of the Russian army personnel was beyond description. Their philosophy was, "have fun with women and then shoot them." Even Stalin had a word for that. He called it "Soldaten Spass," which he encouraged, and translated, means, "soldier fun". The talk among Russian army personnel was, "How many did you rape?" and "How many did you shoot today?" Fortunately, my aunt and sisters escaped those atrocities somehow. We were, as it seemed, always a day ahead, even though when we arrived in Pomaria, they occupied that little town when we first left that night.

Two main things happened in the beginning of March 1945 in Pomaria. One was that Apotheken (pharmacies) could give, without prescription, to women who wanted to commit suicide, any amount of cyanide without limit, as long as supplies were at hand. The second was that the city of Danzig (Gdansk, today) was not as yet occupied by the Russian army. It was a last-minute escape route over the Baltic Sea. Tens of thousands split up from the land route and got to the Baltic Sea as a last resort and made it to the West. Most people that took the sea route also perished there. Actually, tens of thousands perished at sea. The boat was overloaded, and many fell overboard and drowned, never to reach their destination. Somehow, I can't remember exactly, we got on a train. Most trains were just sitting for lack of fuel, but this one took us to the City of Rostock on the Baltic Sea. No sooner had we arrived at the railroad station when bombs were hitting the place. We went in a bomb shelter nearby, and we survived. Day by day we moved on, not exactly knowing where we went.

At last we arrived in the City of Flensburg, the last city before the Danish border. It was in the month of May (I do remember that much), and it was about 9:00 in the morning when the call came, "all on board," and we headed for Denmark. At this time, most refugees were terrified of an unknown future, and there was total confusion among them. Some wished they could go to the western part of Germany, but going to Denmark was out of the question. However, the refugees had no choice but to go on. The train took us to the harbor town of Fredericia, which lay on the eastern part of the mainland. We arrived and stood on the railroad track for about three days, and if memory serves me right, we were there for about one week. I believe the locomotive had run out of coal. We had nothing to eat while standing on that track. I remember on one of the mornings, a Danish man went out to go fishing. He saw me, hungry and bewildered, and he then gave me his sandwiches he had for that day. One had lard and sugar on it, and the other had a scrambled egg. I shared those with the rest of us. It was here in Fredericia that most of the refugees were at wit's end. Utterly hopeless the refugees cried out, "Why did we come here when no one wants us to be here in Denmark? Would to God that we died here rather than to go on!" For me as a child to see the utter distrust and hopelessness was beyond comprehension. It left an indelible imprint on my mind to see the despair when all hope is gone.

Also, while we were standing there, the allied army thought that German U-boats were hiding in the harbor, and they started to bomb that place. It was the British and American air forces that did the bombing at that time. It was also while standing on these tracks that the war had ended, and we saw fireworks that night in celebration of that event. As a kid I didn't really care what went on. Survival was the name of the game. Since it was now the middle of May and school was out, they shipped us to the city of Holstebro, in central Denmark. There we stayed in an empty school building. Vacation had started for the Danish children, and the place was empty. Here we stayed all summer. All classrooms had straw on the floor as beds. I recall hundreds of people in one room. There was no privacy for anyone. The schoolyard was littered with German military hardware and burned-out trucks and tanks, but they served as our playthings. My sister Gerda was always on guard to find food or things that were needed daily. I know my Tante Marta made me my first shoes out of an army uniform, with five or six layers for soles and a double strap on top. They looked like some sort of sandals, but they did the trick! It was better than nothing. I know I was very proud of the shoes, but one time I walked in water, and my aunt spanked me for not taking care of what I had. Life was pretty boring during those summer months since we could never leave the school yard.

In the fall, just before school started again, they shipped us out from there and took us to the northern most part of Denmark, called *Jutland,* to a place called Gedhus. I don't know if it was a city or village. I never found out, but I did find out that the barracks they put us in were from the German occupation of that country. These became our home for the next seventeen months. I don't know the total amount of barracks, but they divided them into four camps. Ours was camp number four, and it had nine barracks in it and about eight hundred people. I had heard that between 6,500 to 7,000 Germans were there in these four camps called Gedhus, so the other camps must have been much larger than ours. One of the camps was in Oksbol. It had 37,000 refugees in it, and I believe it was the largest one in Denmark. Life was pretty lonely up there. The Danes had removed most of the forest there, and the land became almost like a desert, with winds sweeping over the whole area. Worse yet, snow that first winter was over three meters high and made us prisoners in our barracks. Also I recall that each barrack had three rooms, about 30 by 30 feet, and in our room we had eighteen people in it with beds three high and paper blankets for covering. In our camp there was a lady who by profession was a teacher. She organized some sort of school for all the kids. Even my sister Lilli, at about fifteen years of age, was asked to be a teacher's helper for the improvised school. I do not remember, but I might have sat under her tutelage.

Since only woman and children were at this camp, life for them was rough. However I do recall there was one man there. His job was to bring the potatoes to the women to peel every day. Other camps in Denmark had an equal number of men and women. For some reason, we only had the one man. The ladies in our camp were organized, if I recall, barrack to barrack to do the daily cooking for all that were in the camp. Our food consisted mainly of white bread with some potatoes once in a while. Once a week the children at least got some milk soup. There was not much milk in it, because it looked so blue, and we kids would beat it with a stick until it became thick and would not run out of the utensil that we had. The Germans called the milk soup *Magermilch* since all the nutrition was removed from it. Also each of us got about 100 grams of butter a week, and for meat we got some smoked cow utter. Also I recall once in a while we got some hors bologna, which looked so red. Our drink consisted mainly of tea, which I was told was pine needle tea.

I recall that all the ladies became my heroes. In retrospect I recall all the heroic things these ladies did with the little they had. They made us clothes out of old German uniforms, as well as shoes. I believe we also received clothes donated from Sweden, the United States, and perhaps other countries. These ladies never threw anything away. If our socks were old, they unraveled them and sewed new ones. They made sewing needles from an old bicycle wheel that was found. One lady I recall named Mrs. Plikert had a pair of scissors and would cut our hair. After a while, however, we resented her cutting the hair because she took so long. An hour to an hour and a half was the minimum, and we just couldn't hold still that long. Then she became frustrated with us guys. I also recall how the ladies sometimes peeled the potatoes real thick, with the eye still in it, and then we planted them behind the barrack for additional food. Also, some of them became weary of drinking tea, so they made us little kids crawl under the barbed wire and get to the nearby rye and wheat fields, and then they browned the kernels we brought back over a fire. When they were dark brown, we crushed them with stones to make some sort of coffee for them. They seemed to like it! Life in general was pretty boring for us kids, however. We would occupy ourselves by playing in the trenches the German army had dug for protection. These trenches we demolished the first winter we were there for wood to heat our rooms. Those pine branches they had for a wall lining of the trenches and the post for shoring up the walls came in pretty handy for wood. Also the Danes provided little carts for the women to gather some wood in the nearby forest.

The following summer it became apparent that something needed to be done with all the bugs we had in the living area. There was an infestation of a little bug that the Germans called *Wanzen*. It is a small insect like a lady bug except that it has a flat top and is hairy. There are a thousand varieties of these bugs but the ones we had were the "Bedwanzen." They live in every crack and crevice they can find. At night they became very active and would climb over you. They would latch onto your skin and suck your blood. You can only imagine what our skin would look like in the morning. Since the blankets consisted of shredded paper, these bugs were right at home in our beds. The Danes finally thought something needed to be done about the situation, so we had to empty the barracks so they could fumigate the place. The chemical for fumigation was, I believe, DDT, a chemical now banned and for good reason. Both of my sisters got yellow jaundice and got sick from it. Lilli suffered the most from it, and it has also been traced to Gerda's future ailments. At that time little thought was given for the health and safety of people. We had no other place to go, so into the barracks we went at night.

Another area of our existence was some sort of health care. Camp #2 contained all the facilities to take care of ailments. There was a hospital there, an auditorium, and some of the camp's administration. When anyone wanted to go to that camp, we had to tell the guard at the entrance, and when all the people had gathered who wanted to go, then a guard let us go to the other camp. We were not permitted to go there on our own. When one kid got sick from the flu or some other ailment, the whole camp got inoculated for that decease. We kids had a tremendous fear of getting those shots. Those doctors had a long needle and shot wherever in the arm they could. It hurt so much! The kids developed hysteria about it. I saw sometimes nine women holding one child to get the shot. It always became like a slaughter house. We also could not visit the other camps at all, like Camp #1 and #3. Every night at 6 PM a gong would ring, and that was the time we could use the only light we had in the room. It was a 40-watt bulb. Then two hours later it would ring again, and the light had to be extinguished. Otherwise, five minutes later we could expect a bullet to come in our direction. They were very strict.

I think it was in April of 1946 that I came down with a terrible ear infection and had to go in that hospital in Barrack #2. I was there a whole month. They cut my eardrum to ease the pain. My hearing was never the same after that.

Two other barracks I want to mention. One housed the toilets and the other the bath facilities. Every Saturday they would heat the water, and everyone had to take a shower. The shower could hold about fifty people at a time. So the women along with the children would take a shower together. There never was any privacy for the ladies. There was just never a place one could call a private room or corner or a place with a curtain. To this day I marvel how discreetly the ladies handled themselves.

While I was at this refugee camp in Denmark, my first experience of evangelical thought came to us through a German preaching team. Some evangelical and Catholic groups toured Denmark in various camps a couple of month after we arrived there. I don't remember any names, but one of the older folks talked about Martin Niemoller. He was known by some but not by others. Those who did not know him were more critical of him than those who heard of him before. They were critical because he came with a little pomp, while we looked raggedy and poor. I didn't know either way. I did not pay much attention to all that was going on. I was only eight years old, but I learned the great hymn, "Welch Ein Fruend ist Unser Jesus," "What a Friend We Have in Jesus," in German. Also, on some special nights, they would show a movie there.

I also remember a little of that Christmas we had there in 1945. Gedhus, Grove, Karup and Pilis were the four camps that were closely together, only separated by a few miles. In the Grove camp, they started a newspaper called *Grover Nachricten*. In it, they mentioned that Christmas was coming soon, which they called the "Fest of Light.". Many of the older people were familiar with the biblical celebration of Christmas. We had now been at Gedhus for four months, and we settled in our little home. On Christmas Eve, we were all together, "Heilig Abend" in German. The older people called this Christmas, "Christmas behind barbed-wire." Many of us felt our freedom was gone forever. And our destiny: who knew? All in all there were 250,000 German refugees in over 1,100 camps in Denmark. Many felt that criminals in the jails had it better than the German refugees behind the barbed wire.

We didn't have anything but each other and with the other eighteen people in our room in barrack #4, we sang those nice German Christmas carols. I know most of the older people got homesick. We younger ones didn't really understand what it all was about. However, the Danes had given each child an orange and two little sticks of Plexiglas for a candle. We lit them and in a few moments all was gone. Today, I sit here with tears in my eyes and think of that day we celebrated Christmas. I think that was the best Christmas I ever had, with nothing. I think now how Jesus must have felt. The Creator of the whole universe, coming in human form to this earth, lying with nothing of importance in a stable, with only the most lowly people to greet Him. I will probably never forget that Christmas as long as I live. For some reason, even as a child, it had a tremendous impact on my life. I can still see all of us sitting on those wooden benches and wooden tables as if it was yesterday.

The summer in 1946 was still very boring for us kids. However, we occupied ourselves with was building kites. I can't remember where we got some large sheets of paper, but we got it from somewhere. The kites we made were huge, like 1.5 meter (5 ft. tall). For string we made lines from burlap bags. We would sit for days at a time and unravel each individual thread and then braid them into long lines, so long, that a five-foot kite looked like a little dot in the sky. The ever-present wind in the Jutland plain was ideal for kite flying. In fact most of the kites had to be held by more than one kid. I remember when one child was lifted up from the ground by one and had to release the kite; otherwise, he would have gone up into the heavens. That sport occupied us most of that summer.

Chapter 4

A Family Reunited

Help me then in every tribulation so to trust your
promises O Lord.
That I lose not faith's sweet consolation offered me
within your holy Word.
Help me Lord, when toil and trouble meeting, e'er to
take as from a father's hand.
One by one the days, the moments fleeting,
till I reach the promised land.

Carolina Sandell Berg, 1865

The fall of 1946 came (my sister recollects better than I),
and the Danes notified the camp population that whoever
could find a family member or relative in West Germany and West
Berlin could proceed to leave the camp when enough people found
a place to return. They would ship those people out as transportation
became available. My thought here was that the Danes negotiated
with the Allied authorities to take some refugees off their hands.
That was good news for us. At the age of nine, I cared nothing about
the political situation, only that our time here would end. Our Tante

Marta had an aunt whose name was Martha Fischer. She must have moved before the final days of the war to the West from the eastern part of Germany, and she also had her address, the only address of anybody of our family. She wrote to her. I believe with the help of the German Red Cross, she located my Tante Emmi, Marta's sister, who had fled to Berlin and, guess what? She located our father! I can vaguely remember when we got the first mail from both of them, but I do remember the letter from our father because Tante Martha told us all the details of it. In it father wrote us that he had survived the whole war in Russia, became a prisoner of war by the Americans in Germany, had escaped from them, and made his home on the Mosel area of Germany. Also, he said that he had remarried and had a son and a second child on the way. This was naturally a hard pill to swallow for an eight-and-a-half-year old. But it was our father whom we had not seen since my mother's funeral in February of 1941. Now it was toward the end of 1946. He didn't know we were still alive; neither did we know that he was alive, and so he started a new life for himself. I can't remember my sisters' reaction at that time, but I was excited but also a little apprehensive. Again, it was another unknown.

Finally, the day came when enough people had found someone in West Germany or West Berlin that a train load of people could leave Denmark. I remember that we were among the first to leave Gedhus. Mrs. Plickert, the one who cut my hair, finally left Denmark in almost 1949 because she and her family had no place to go. They were among the last to leave. At this age I cannot recall all that we had to do, but the day came that we actually packed the few belongings we had. Then, as I recall, on December 5, 1946, we left Gedhus, Denmark. I don't remember where we boarded the train, but we actually made it. I do remember that our car was somewhere in the middle of the train, because at the end they had a few freight cars for belongings.

It was slow going I recall; every day a few miles. Today a trip like that can be made in a day, but it took us almost three weeks to get to the city of Worms in Germany. It's in the southwestern part of Germany. I don't know why the city of Worms was chosen for the destination. However the weeks on that train took their toll on us. I recall that after the first week of traveling, that the bearings of our car ran hot, and the car had to be removed. Naturally they had no car to replace ours, so they shoved us in one of those freight cars in the back, and for the next few weeks we had to endure the freezing condition that existed in December. Some train stations had some warm soup for us, but most of the time we had nothing that I remember. I had an old canteen bottle and at some stops of the train, I went to the locomotive and got some dirty, but hot water, from the reservoir of the locomotive. It would keep me warm. The only shoes that I had were the ones my Tante Martha made me out of some German Army uniforms. They were like sandals. Over the course of three weeks, my feet started to freeze and became frostbitten. I must tell you, however, that we were eighty people in the little freight car, packed like sardines.

We arrived at Worms on Christmas Eve 1946. It was late that day, and we had no place to go. We spent Christmas Eve all huddled together with our few belongings in the little corner of the freight car. I don't know if we received something to eat that night or not. The next day we were allowed to leave the freight car, and the rail-road authorities put us in a fairly large building that must have been something like a gymnasium. The building was not too badly dam-aged from the war. All the passengers from the train were inside, about eight hundred people. Again, it was like a slaughterhouse. There was nowhere to sit, nowhere to lie down, small kids were crying, and there was more commotion than you can imagine.

We endured that night there. The next day the authorities divided the people and took some to a former hotel, which was bombed out on the upper floors, but resembled a former ball room. That is where the authorities put us. We were the last people to enter that room, so we were very close to the door. I recall that we took turns sleeping. Here we were not sardines but herring, with just a little more room!

I don't know who notified our father to come and pick us up, but I recall the next day he was in Worms. Some authority, perhaps from the Red Cross (but I don't know exactly), made an announcement and told the refugees to be ready when someone came to pick us up. It was in the afternoon that a man came through the door and looked for a good while to find someone he knew. After about some five to ten minutes, he left when he didn't recognize anyone he was looking for. Tante Martha, sisters Lilli and Gerda, wondered who this man could be. I also looked at him but sort of brushed away the thought that the man could be our father. A few minutes later that man must have second thoughts. He came back into the room to look for his family.

Once again he looked over all the heads, because most people were standing. There simply was no room to sit down. Finally the man turned again for the door, but before he left, he turned around, put his two hands over his mouth and hollered, "Is there a family by the name Schakat here?" Well, at that time we all knew this was our father! The strain of war, the uncertainties of the problems at hand, neither father nor his sister, our Tante Martha, nor my sisters Lilli and Gerda, recognized him. I, being the youngest, had no clue what my father looked like.

No one can really fathom the moment of reunion. All of our hearts broke. A father seeing his children once again and a sister seeing her brother again was a special time. It must have been like a resurrection from the dead for the father and his children. This moment is just as vivid to me now after sixty-five years as the time it took place—weeping and crying, crying and laughing all at the same time.

The last time I had seen my father was at my mother's funeral on February 5, 1941 when he held me on his arm, a three-and-a-half-year-old kid. I was so proud of him then, because he had brought me some chocolate and a pair of Russian felt boots and gave me flowers to throw on mother's grave. All of that came back almost at in instant. A child's features change dramatically from a little guy to an almost nine year old. No wonder father had a hard time recognizing any one of us, and we him. He was now so skinny. Being an American prisoner of war less than two years prior and having to start life all over again at age forty-three took a tremendous toll on him. Not remembering father's earlier physique, I believe he never became his old self again the rest of his life, dying early at the age of sixty-four.

Chapter 5

Ernst am Mosel

Fear not little flock, He goeth ahead, your Shepherd
selecteth the path you must tread. The waters of
Marah He'll sweeten for thee, He drank all the bitter
in Gethsemane.

Fear not little flock, whatever your lot, He enters all
rooms the doors being shut.
He never forsakes, He never is gone, so count on His
presence in darkness and dawn.

Paul Rader, *Only Believe* (1921)

*A*fter this reunion, father took us to the train station to
head to our new home in Ernst on the Mosel River.
Train connections were very limited at that time. We left Worms
later that afternoon and arrived in Mainz or Koblenz—I cannot
remember for sure—late at night. I think it was Koblenz, which is
the city where the Rhein and Mosel rivers meet. We stayed overnight in some bunker right near the railroad station. Everywhere one
looked there was bombed out buildings, streets and facilities. The

fact that a train even made some headway at that time was quite a wonder, to say the least.

The next day we took another train to Cochem on the Mosel River. It is about fifty kilometers from Koblenz to Cochem, but I remember it took a considerable amount of time to get there. Cochem is about five kilometers from Ernst. If my memory serves me right, we walked home. During the trip from Koblenz to Cochem, father instructed us how we should deal with our new mother. He told us that this lady will be addressed as "Mother." I think my sisters had a little more apprehension than I, since I had never dealt with my own mother, as she died young, and I can never remember a time when mother was home. Since she was constantly sick and very often in the hospital, I never remembered her. Even now as I am seventy-five, I somehow long to know what mother sounded like, how she laughed and cried and did things with us. But now I had a stepmother and was to call her "Mother." This was a little strange to me. Then a German proverb came to my mind that says, "A little tree bends better than an old one."

We came to Ernst shortly in the afternoon. Father introduced us to our new mother and his son, my new brother Werner. Mother was pregnant with their second child. (I remember the first letter we got from father in Denmark when he mentioned it.) She greeted us warmly and accepted us in the new family. As a young fellow, one accepts new surroundings quickly. Again I remembered the proverb, "A little tree just bends better than an old one."

It was New Year's Eve 1946 when we arrived in Ernst. As I mentioned earlier, the trip from Koblenz to Cochem took several hours. It was a fairly good ride, but what exited me most of all was the pretty scenery of the Mosel valley. I had a faint idea of what castles looked like, but now I saw them in reality. Most of the castles are in ruins, not from the last war, but from the many armies that marched through Germany in the last 800–1000 years. The last army was that of Napoleon, and it was the worst and most destructive in the eighteenth century. Whatever was still standing at the time was totally destroyed by him. The castle in Cochem was still intact. It was built in the twelfth century and rebuilt in the eighteenth. I remember making several comments to my father about it, but he didn't have too much knowledge of the castles, either.

What took place the rest of the day or that evening, or whether we celebrated New Year's Eve is presently blank in my mind.

I was now nine-and-a-half years old. In January 1947, father enrolled my sisters and me in the public school in Ernst. The town of Ernst had at that time a population of about six hundred. The school building was in the center of town, next to the church on one side, and the teacher's house on the other. Ernst itself is an old town, mentioned in archives from at least the eleventh and early twelfth century. It was basically divided into "Ober" and "Nieder," Upper and Lower Ernst. Up to that point I had no formal education to say the least, except the few weeks before we left home. Whatever I learned, I learned from the informal teaching of the woman in the refugee camp and from my sister, Lilli, who was fifteen at the time. My recollection of the class was that there were about eighty children in the room. Grades 5–8 were taught in the morning from 8 –AM to 12 PM, and grades 1–4 were taught in the afternoon from 1 to 4 PM. There was only one teacher, and his name was Herman Stein. Even though the size of the class was rather big, Herr Stein was in perfect control, and the children's behavior was impeccable. Not a word was spoken by anyone! Lehrer (teacher) Stein taught every subject, whether music or arithmetic or literature. I remember when I was finally in the eighth grade, I had to memorize Poet Schiller's "Lied von der Glocke," translated as "The Song of the Bell," in its entirety. It had eighteen pages in our reading book, and I had to recite it before the whole class. If you missed more than a few words, you had to study and memorize it until you knew every word. He was so thorough in his teaching that to this day, sixty-four years later, I still remember most of it.

School in those days was not only classroom education but life-lessons as well. Here was one that I will never forget: I remember one day I decided to go home during lunch time. Our house was just a little distance from school along a narrow path. There was a garden that someone had right behind the school. I saw a nice, ripe tomato right along the fence. I took one and ate it, not realizing that the owner saw me grabbing it. When I returned a few minutes later, the owner had gone to Lehrer (teacher) Stein and told him what I had done. He confronted me, and I admitted that I took it. Lehrer

Stein made me go out by the Mosel River and get a willow rod, and when I returned, I had to go the front of the class, lean over the first bench and proceed to get a real good whipping. But that was not all! By the time father got home that evening, Lehrer Stein had gone to him and told him what I had done. Well, you can imagine. I got a second whipping. I never forgot that lesson. Just don't take what is not yours.

Another thing that Lehrer Stein made me do ended up a little more comical. Being in eighth grade now, sometimes we had to do some personal favors for him. One day he told me and my friend, Robert Andrae, to kill a chicken for his wife for supper that day. Herr Stein's house was right next to the school building, and the chickens were right next to that. Between Robert and me, we decided that I would catch the chicken and Robert would kill it. I held the chicken on the wood block and Robert took the ax and cut its head off. Little did I realize that an animal still had some life in it even when its head was cut off. I let the chicken go, and lo and behold, it flew up to the first story and landed right on Mrs. Steins' bedding she had on the window to air out, a typical German custom. Now we had to go to Mr. Stein and tell him what happened. Here were two guys now that were scared to death. We did not get spanked but got a real lesson about killing chickens and the importance of preserving fine linens. The outside casing of a down comforter can be rather easily replaced with a new one, simply by transferring the feathers in a new casing. Nevertheless, I remember the incident to this day. The four years that I went to school in Ernst were rather good years.

The region of Northwest Germany is predominately Roman Catholic. Since my father's side of the family was refugees, we were the only three persons in town that were Protestant. Every day all the kids in school had to go to Mass, including myself. The local priest came twice a week to school and taught Catholic catechism. Since we went to school six days a week, I had to go on Saturdays to Cochem, five kilometers away, to the Lutheran Church for Protestant catechism. So every Saturday I went all day to Cochem. It was in the Lutheran Church in Cochem that I was confirmed later in 1951 in that faith.

Chapter 6

Contact from America:
A Glimmer of Hope

Be not dismayed what'er betide, God will take of you; Beneath His wings of love abide, God will take care of you.

No matter what may be the test, God will take care of you; lean weary one upon His breast, God will take care of you.
Civillia D. Martin, *God Will Take Care of You,* 1904

*T*he year 1947 started out sort of bad in many ways. Besides starting school, the first thing I had to do was get medical attention for my frozen and frostbitten feet. The weeks of travel from Denmark to Germany in an ice cold freight car took their toll on my feet. I left Denmark with the only shoes that my Tante Marta made me from an old army uniform, which I mentioned that earlier. These were sort of like sandals, certainly not for the cold winter. I had hardly any feeling left when we arrived in the city of Worms, where our father picked us up. There were not too many doctors in Germany after the war. Father, however, found one that would treat my feet, and in a few weeks I was almost completely healed. It was an extremely cold winter that year; even the Mosel River was frozen solidly, with big ice chunks still lying on the shore until May.

The next bad thing that happened was the sickness of my sister Lilli. When we left Pomeria that frightened night and went through that bad field, the same one that my Grandma lost her shoes in, Lilli did something to her hip that never left her. The rest of our flight and the time in Denmark only aggravated the situation without any medical treatment. I believe it was April when Lilli entered the hospital in Ebernach near Cochem on the Mosel River. Lilli never came home again, after special hospitals near Koblenz am Rhine. She died in August 1948 after this long illness. I was now eleven years old, and her death affected me terribly. Even at that age I started to value how precious life is. (I'll speak more on her death later.)

As the months went on, it became apparent that not only was the winter extremely cold, but the summer was extremely hot. It was so hot, in fact, that few local people had ever experienced such extreme weather. We planted potatoes in the spring, but nothing grew. We had two cows, one black and white, called Lotte, and the other brown, called Braune. We had a hard time keeping them alive. I took both cows every day after school to the forest to graze, besides going to the vineyards to pick dandelions for food. By the time fall and winter came around, both cows were only living skeletons, but they did give us a little milk. We also had a goat, which was closely attached to our mother. No one but her had that privilege to milk her. Therefore, she could never be away for a long time when milking time came around. This goat was sort of funny. During milking she always lifted her rear leg up and turned her head around to watch mother milking her. No wonder no one but mother could milk her!

Even we had a hard time surviving. We lived at this period in the French Zone. Every village had a French Gendarme stationed. Every little amount of food we had, like eggs or some milk, we had to give daily to him, which left us with practically nothing to eat even though we had a little farmland to grow things. My sister Gerda, bless her heart, would go at such a young age to the Eifel Mountain, the mountain range to the left of the Mosel River, to trade a few bottles of wine for some flour. My stepmother would make something out of it and also would bake some bread, so we knew every day what we had for dinner. It was always the same. The usual water, some noodles, here and there an onion, and perhaps on Sundays a few potatoes. This went on the whole summer until early fall. By then my father would venture into the British Zone, with a special made jacket that would hold several bottles of wine, and he went to Bremerhafen on the North Sea to get some Herring. For ten bottles of wine he got 300 herrings. From then on we ate herring morning, noon and night, and in every way imaginable: smoked, fried, rolled, and fried again. This was our only meat, and we ate everything but the eyes and the tail. My sister Thea (she was the daughter of my stepmother's first husband) was the only one who could not stomach herring, but in the end she, too, would eat them, but not the milk and the row of the fish. This meager food supply caused all of us to be very skinny. I weighed, at ten-and-one-half years old, a total of fifty-three pounds and my father had gone down from 170 to 135 pounds.

Also my father started a business that year. Since he was a trained butcher, he had an interest in buying cow hides, furs from animals like goats and sheep, and also hair from pigs. He would go from one butcher shop to the next in order to buy whatever these butcher shops had from slaughtering animals for the week. Every week he would make his rounds visiting the same butchers, whether they were on the Mosel area or the Eifel or Hunsrueck mountains.

Once the businesses got to know him they would save all he was interested to buy, so his business grew after a short time. I don't recall what father paid for all these skins. I think it was rather cheap. Whenever he expected lots of hides, he would take me along after school. Cow hides are very heavy. However, these required lot of work when he came home. All the hides had to be salted and stored until he had enough to take them to the tanners, and the furs had to be dried.

Saturdays in the spring was always a busy time for slaughtering young goats. Young goat meat is a delicacy in Germany. Father would leave early Saturday mornings and come home late at night. Then on Sunday mornings it was my job was to hang them out to dry, usually over one hundred to one hundred fifty and sometimes even more. After that I had to go to church to Cochem, five kilometers by bike. Father would not drive his little truck on Sundays. The truck that father had been an early production of a German revival in the auto industry. It had three wheels, one in front and two in the rear. On top of the front wheel was a small motor. I think it had only 650 cc, and a chain drove the front wheel. It was called "TEMPO." The top speed was a meager forty to fifty miles per hour. Father had a habit of down-shifting when he was almost home and our dog would begin to bark. When he did, we knew dad was almost home.

The business also had a few perks. Since he came in contact with a lot of butchers and also with some farmers, bartering was the name of the game in those days. One product was exchanged for another.

Farmers in the Eifel Mountains had farm products, and we had a little wine. So it was toward the winter that he would trade wine for potatoes, so our food supply started to improve a little. Now we had herring along with potatoes. What a treat!

Father had always an eye for some other venture or some thought of something out of the ordinary. Traveling one day he came across a shepherd that grazed along the Mosel River. Father thought that many sheep would make good fertilizer for our back yard behind the house. The lot was all fenced in, so it made for a perfect accommodation for about two hundred sheep. So in the evening came two hundred sheep in our back yard. There so much noise and bleating that even the neighbors complained. The next morning the sheep left and went to graze along the river. In the evening, they all came back. The yard looked real muddy and trodden by all those sheep. There was only one shepherd for all those animals. In the evening the shepherd got up and said he had to make a phone call. Father told him he could use our phone (we had gotten one recently). But he said he would rather use the pay phone instead. As our luck went, he never came back! We did not know where he was from or who owned those sheep. It took two days to find the owner, who was in the lower Rhein area near Cologne. Now for the next few days I became a shepherd until the owners came and took the sheep from us. I learned a few things about the keeping of sheep in the few days. Our little yard was very well fertilized and trampled. My father learned to be more careful of whom he asked to come over.

One of the turning points of that year and my future life was that somehow we made contact with our relatives in America. There were ten children from my mother's side, four of whom immigrated to America. I believe they arrived between 1911 and 1918. Their names were Otto, Ida, Helen, and Ottilie Tiepel. I think it was Helen and Ottilie that remembered that my mother had children but did not know what happened to them. Through the Red Cross they found us and established correspondence with us. Naturally we were very happy about that contact. In one of our first letters, father requested if they could send some penicillin for Lilli because the doctor had said to us if he only had penicillin he could help Lilli tremendously. By the end of September we got a care package with the medicine and some coffee, Crisco, and some clothing, which was greatly appreciated. (The medicine actually arrived a few days after Lilli died.) Over the next few years we got several care packages with some food and clothing; most of it was too big, and mother had to alter many pieces. The year 1947 ended with the first Christmas together as a family since 1939. It too was a very sparse celebration. I only remembered that mother had baked some cookies, and each of us got an orange, which was so precious to me that I did not eat it for a long time. By then it had shriveled up. I think it was almost March by the time I ate what was left.

Chapter 7

Lilli

Whate'er my God ordains is right: Though now this cup, in drinking, May bitter seem to my faint heart, I take it, all unshrinking. My God is true; each morn anew Sweet comfort yet shall fill my heart, And pain and sorrow shall depart.

Whate'er my God ordains is right: Here shall my stand be taken; Though sorrow, need, or death be mine, Yet I am not forsaken. My Father's care is round me there; He holds me that I shall not fall: And so to Him I leave it all.

Samuel Rodegast, 1676 (*Was Gott Tut, das ist wohlgetan*)

The year 1948 looked a little more promising on many fronts. The German economy started to improve as the building boom started and industries got on their feet again. By May, they dropped rationing cards on select items like butter and sugar. Also Germany got new money. The Reichsmark was replaced by the Deutsche Mark, DM. The Reichsmark was worthless long before it was replaced. I remember buying a loaf of bread and paying over 500 Reichsmark for it. I also treated myself to some candy. One wrapped piece would cost over ten Reichsmark. However one piece would last me over a week. Every day I would suck on it for about five minutes; then I would wrap it up for my pleasure the next day. I was very disciplined in doing that and hid it so no one could find it.

Even our two cows put on a little weight but remained skinny. However Lotte, the black and white one, died in early summer. She was my favorite. I remember going in the stall to feed her that morning before school and she was lying all stretched out with her eyes rolling. Father butchered her for some needed meat, since the French Gendarme didn't want a dead cow's meat. Father made some liverwurst and blood sausage and made some head cheese out of it.

My sister Lilli, in the meantime, became increasingly sicker. They transferred her from the hospital near Koblenz where she was for several months to a sanitarium in the Eifel Mountain where the air was clean, with lots of forest around it. The reason for that move was that Lilli had developed tuberculosis and would have to be away from the rest of the people. This was toward the end of July. A few weeks after that our whole family went to visit her along with our pastor from the church in Cochem who then administered the Lord's Supper to her. We all saw that Lilli got increasingly weaker, but she maintained a positive attitude despite the pain and suffering. I remember leaving the room several times because I could not comprehend that she would perhaps not be with us very much longer. We all came home sad that day, because we knew that her young life would soon be over. I remember how the pastor comforted me on the way home and told me that we all need to prepare for such a day because no one would stay on earth forever. I was eleven years old now and had to act like a grown-up to understand the meaning of life. It was only less than two weeks after our visit that Lilli succumbed to her sickness.

Lilli had a roommate that was with her already in the hospital near Koblenz and was also transferred to the Eifel hospital. I forget her name. She wrote to my sister Gerda of the last few days of Lilli's life. Her lungs had filled with fluid, and her breathing became excruciatingly hard, and yet she thanked her doctors and nurses for having been so good to her. She also shared with her roommate the personal faith she had in God, which I thought was so remarkable for her age at eighteen. She always had such a caring personality. On Sunday, September 5, 1948, Lilli went to be with her Lord. Sunday morning and through the day Lilli expressed to her roommate that this would be her last day on earth and remarked to her, "My little sister Emmi died on Sunday, and my dear mother died on Sunday, and I will die today also." So in the evening she was gone.

I cannot remember how we got the body of Lilli home, but I do remember where we stored it until the funeral. It was in the building across the street from our house that belonged to the Vintners Co-op that our family belonged to. The vineyards we owned had approximately 35,000 stocks of wine plants at the time which was not enough to make a living, so quite a few Vintners belonged to the Co-Up. They had this rather large room where the vine presses stood. This room served as our funeral home for the next few days, because funeral homes were not heard of at that time. Bodies were not embalmed the way we know it today. They used just a pine casket because graves did not stay in the cemetery any longer than thirty to forty years at the most. The cemetery in Ernst is less than an acre. When it is full they start from the next end to bury people and dig former graves back up.

Father took her death very hard. Being a former soldier he never showed much emotion, but this time was different. I remember he took me to this room one afternoon and he just broke down like a baby, both of us standing next to the coffin crying. Having lost a daughter, Emmi, at age six, and then his first wife at age thirty-three and now his oldest daughter dead at age eighteen, this was a tremendous loss to him. (Emmi had died before I was born.)

Lilli was then buried in the cemetery of Ernst, officiated by our Lutheran pastor Dr. Erwin teReh, who was our beloved pastor at the Evangelical Church in Cochem. I remember him as a godly man who tirelessly rebuilt the congregation after the war. No task was too big or small for him. He did all of his pastoral duties on an old pre-war motorcycle, come rain or shine. I was sort of intrigued by that old thing and the way he dressed up when he rode it. Being eleven years old, I dreamed of riding one of those things someday. Dr. teReh later became my instructor in Lutheran catechism for my Confirmation in 1951, although he did not confirm me, having retired the year before that. This man really influenced my young life. He took special interest in me because of my troubled background. He always made sure I understood every word in Luther's Catechism and that I was able to recite everything. I think he planted the seed in my young life that later influenced me to become a Christian because I always wanted to be like him, doing every task cheerfully, never complaining, never carrying a grudge.

The year 1948 had another important happening. We got mail from America that my grandma, from my mother's side, whom none of us kids knew, had flown to America at the age of seventy-seven. It happened the same day we buried Lilli, unknown to us at the time. Four of my mother's brothers and sisters had come to America between the years of 1911 and 1918. Not only did they search for us after the war but also for their mother, who they found in a refugee camp in Germany. The details of her getting there are at present vague to me, but it was the Lange family and Adolph, my mother's brother and family, that brought her out of Lithuania. She was so weak for the flight that she needed several units of blood before she could fly to America. However, she lived with my uncle Otto in Pittsburgh and with my aunt Ida in Michigan and with my aunts Helen and Ottilie in Cincinnati for a total of almost ten years. She died in Cincinnati at the age of eighty-eight years, being of clear mind about fifteen minutes before she was gone. (I will mention more of her when I finally get to America and more details of the Lange family).

The rest of the year started to improve in many ways: the German economy revived, and our lives started to improve as well. The French occupation eased up for us also. No longer did we have to give to them some of our farm products. However, the school children had to get snails that were plentiful in the vineyards for the French. Every time it rained these creatures would be crawling everywhere in the vineyards, and to the French, they were a delicacy, so it was the school children's job to collect them. We sort of liked to get off from school for a few hours to collect these creatures for them. It did not take long for about sixty kids to have quite a few of them. For us it was better than giving our milk and eggs to them.

Earlier in the year my Tante Marta left us to pursue her own life, having raised me from age three and before when my mother was sick and finally died. Lilli, Gerda, and I were from that time under her care. During the time we left our home in East Prussia, the flight that ended up in Denmark, and our reuniting with my father, she took us under her wing, so to speak. She was more than a mother to me. She always stood tall in my mind, having never married to devote so many years of her life to raise her brother's children. The only reward she got from my father was some form of resentment. I was too young to see it but I sensed that father did not like her. It became so bad between them that Marta finally left home. She got a job as a domestic for an industrialist in the city of Alf on the Mosel River, about forty kilometers upriver from Ernst. I visited her many times in Alf; however, father would never give me any money to do so. The train fare would cost six DM, and to raise the money I would go in the orchards and pick rotten and fallen apples and plums and take them to a man who bought them to make some brandy type of drink. He paid actually good money for them. Four pails full would get me the money I needed. But since the old man could not see very well, I would fill the bottom of my pails with water to increase the weight. Bad boy! One devises many tricks when in a jam, and that is one I remember to this day. I am sorry to say that it also became my way to make money to buy shoes for Sundays. Father did not believe in supplying items other than for work. How we got shoes and other clothing items did not bother him. My stepmother would take the items we got from America and alter them to fit my small frame. Often I felt like I was a stepchild the way I was treated by my father. When I think of those years I would rather forget them, but they are part of my life, and I have to live with those memories. I was now ten-and-one-half years old and weighed only sixty pounds. I remember the weight so well because my neighbor friend weighted sixty kilograms. That was 120 pounds. His name was Manfred, and he added some brighter moments in my life. We both loved to run the 60- and 100-meter dash. The 60-meter we did in 6.7 seconds and the 100-meter in 11.2 seconds, and we were both were happy with that speed. Manfred would always laugh when I ran because my legs were so little and it seemed like a blitz (lightening) to him. Manfred was also good at playing soccer. It always seemed he had time for a lot of things that I didn't. My father saw to it that I always had a job to do after school that prevented me from participating in any sport. He would find the craziest things to do just to keep me occupied at something other than things I would enjoy.

One day he came home with another of his great ideas. He thought that ice cream might be a good money maker during summer. Perhaps someone in Ernst had thought about selling it, but no one had acted upon it. Somewhere he found an old ice cream churn, and he thought, "That's it!" We had an old barn across the street that was part of the rented buildings we had. My father believed he could use that spot for an ice cream store. However, like anything he under-took, it involved work, not only for himself, but also for others. (That meant me!) So then, every Sunday morning *I* had to get up early in the morning and go to Cochem to get ice, because he would never drive the truck on Sundays. The ice sticks were one meter long, twenty-five centimeters high ,and ten centimeters wide, each weighing about twenty-five pounds. Dad needed four of those to produce his specialty. That's one hundred pounds of ice! Remember, I only weighed sixty pounds, and I had to bring those ice sticks back on my bicycle. Then, I had to chop them up and get the machine going. By 10 AM I had to go back to Cochem to go to church! After dinner the ice cream was ready, and he took me with him wherever a festival was going on. For that however, he took the truck because he made money. He would take me all over the area. Then, when we arrived, he would disappear, and we never saw him until evening.

For all that work I got a meager 50 cents, which he thought was good money. I remember my father and my stepmother fighting over this business like cats and dogs. My stepmother did win one part of the argument: I received a raise of 1 DM! This went on for two summers and I was only twelve years old.

The next few years, 1949 and 1950, were basically uneventful. It was mostly school and then work after school. However, we continued the correspondence with our American relatives, who would send us many care packages. Things were still not the way we wished. The food supply was getting better, and certain items were no longer on stamps. But as a whole we struggled along with many things. I remember father requesting patches and glue so that we could fix our bicycle inner tubes. It was items like these that were in such small supply and simply not available. Gasoline was one item we could only buy in small amounts. At one time my father had a chance to buy an American car from someone. I don't know who sold him the car, but it was a Willys Overland. It had six cylinders and would run, but we had no gasoline! At that time there was a technology developed where a car could be converted to burn wood. The Overland was a candidate for it. The trunk could be converted into an oven. Piping went over the roof to the front to an evaporator or chamber of some sort where the superheated wood-gas was stored. But the final product, I believe, was methanol gas. In the winter it took forever to get it going. In the summer it wasn't as bad. After the oven was lit with a one-foot-long match, we had to wait about ten minutes until it got warm enough for the engine to do something. The four liters of gasoline we got per week, about one gallon, would start the car for few minutes; then the methanol was ready to switch over, and hopefully the Jeepster would run. It was a real pain, not only to get it going, but also that it required we take a lot of wood along for the trip. I only remember a fifty-kilometer trip took almost three eighty-pound bags of wood. However, father was proud of this thing because he could pull a trailer with it and above all else, no one had a six-cylinder car in town. (I don't know if my explanation on this technology is completely correct, but one can investigate it further. Remember I was not even thirteen years old yet.) It was sometime in 1950 when the restriction of gasoline was lifted and also the end of the Willys Overland Jeepster.

Chapter 8

My Word Will Not
Return unto Me Void

Evening and morning, sunset and dawning, wealth,
peace and gladness, comfort in sadness, These are
Thy works; all the glory be Thine! Times without
number, awake or in slumber, Thine eye observes
us, from danger preserves us, Causing Thy mercy
upon us to shine.

Father, O hear me, pardon and spare me; Calm all
my terrors, blot out my errors, that by Thine eyes
they may no more be scanned. Order my goings,
direct all my doings; as it may please Thee retain or
release me; all I commit to Thy fatherly hand.

Paul Gerhardt (*Die Guldne Sonne,* 1666)

*T*he year 1951 rolled around the corner, and quite a few things
happened in my life. As I wrote earlier, on Saturdays I had
Protestant religious training in Cochem. The time had come that I
would be confirmed in the Lutheran faith. That training consisted
of learning Luther's catechism, many parts of the Bible, lots of
Psalms, numerous hymns, and Lutheran thought. The Sunday before

confirmation day was the great test. The church was packed; every seat was taken. I can't positively remember how many students were in the confirmation class there that year. The number sixteen sticks in my memory.

The pastor would ask all of us questions of the things we had learned. I was asked three different questions in the course of the service. The first one was Luther's explanation of several of the Ten Commandments. The second was to recite Psalm 103 in its entirety. The third was to recite Paul Gerhard's great hymn "Die Guldne Sonne" ("The Golden Sun"). It had twelve verses to it, and I knew them all. At the end the pastor announced that I was the best one of all that participated. I must say I was very proud of myself. The following Sunday was Easter, and I was confirmed in the Lutheran Church. Father and mother had good food prepared that I hadn't seen in a long time. Many of my relatives came, namely Tante Marta, my uncle Fritz, and family and other family from stepmother's side. Also, my sister Gerda came from Konstace am Bodensee (Lake Constance in English). I received my first watch and a pocket Lutheran hymnal with my name engraved on it as gifts for my confirmation. I was very proud of those gifts. Two weeks later I got two more gifts from my aunts in America. Aunt Helen sent me $5, and Aunt Ottilie sent me $25. That was $127.50 DM at the time. My father had a custom suit made for me. There was a tailor who lived at the end of our property. He measured me and made me a new suit for my confirmation. It fit perfectly! It was dark and had pinstripes on it, and I thought it looked rather good on me! Since we were a family of modest means, I thought the expensive suit was a little overkill, but I wore it with pride. The confirmation went well. My newly found wealth did not sit well with my father. He started to grumble and insinuate that the money I received from America should be used to pay for the suit. I told him that was a gift from my aunts and that it was given to me personally. My father believed that since I did not give him the money for the suit that meant I was a disobedient son. The following week, having just come home from church, I went upstairs to change my suit before we ate dinner. His anger became so great that he came upstairs and beat me up so bad I thought I would die. My stepmother heard the commotion upstairs and came up and joined my father's beating of me. My sister Gerda was still at home from her vacation for my confirmation. She came upstairs and they beat her up as well. She was already eighteen years old, but age did not matter to them. It was like a slaughterhouse. I found out later that father paid 250 DM. for the suit and wanted me to contribute a hefty share to it. In the end, I won and did not give him the money.

About that time I saw an ad in the newspaper from a bicycle company that sold bikes for $120 DM, and I told the whole family what I was about to do: order myself a bike. In a few weeks I was the proud owner of a brand new bike. It was red and shiny, and I rode all over Ernst with it!

Later that summer, my father began to comment that I was not growing as I should. I was now fourteen years old, and I only weighed sixty-three pounds. Father thought I should not be this small, so he recommended that I should go get some rest and recuperation, but he did not know where that would be. He came up with the idea to place an ad in the newspaper to see if some childless couple would consider taking in a fourteen-year-old boy for a few weeks on a farm or wherever. Interestingly enough, we got two replies: one from about thirty kilometers down the Mosel River and the other from the Eifel Mountains, about ninety kilometers away. I chose the Eifel area, since I lived on the Mosel anyway.

We contacted the people and told them the day I would come. The family was Johann Gerhards and his wife Anna. They had no children, but the man's sister Katharina also lived there. My father could have easily taken me there with his truck, but he refused. The day came when I had to leave, so I took my new bike, a few clothes, and my Lederhosen and left early that morning. Going up the mountain required that I push the bike more than I rode it. I had no map other than the instruction father gave me, and I had no sandwich and no water because he thought I would arrive in three hours. After about five hours, I came to some "no-man's land" where the road split, and there was no sign to any town. My scripture verse came to mind: "My ways are not your ways." Nevertheless, I was a little frightened. I chose the right fork instead of the left. It was a long way when I looked and saw a forest all the way up, which meant

I had to push the bike all the way up the mountain. When I finally reached the top I saw, in the distance, a man coming up the other side, also pushing his bike. I was so glad to see another person and I waited until the person came up the hill. We introduced ourselves to each other and started to ride our bikes. As we rode along, the man asked me where I was going. I said, "To Mannebach." He didn't talk too much, but after a while he said, "I too go to Mannebach; just follow me." As we were riding along he then asked me what my purpose was in going to Mannebach. I told him that I was going to the family of Johann Gerhards. We rode along perhaps another thirty minutes when he said to me, "Well, what do you think? I'm Johann Gerhards"? No one can imagine how I felt at that moment as tears came to my eyes. I couldn't believe what was going on. I then asked him how far it was to Mannebach, and he said almost another hour. So we rode along and got there at 3 PM, eight hours from when I left home! I was so hungry, thirsty, and tired. Johann introduced me to Anna, his wife, and Katharina, his sister. We had a light lunch and right after Johann told me what my job would be: tending the four cows and two oxen, but mainly the cows. They also had a number of pigs and chickens. Their farm had about forty acres, but all the fields grassland, and pasture were scattered all over. I remember about twenty-two different locations in all. Right after lunch he showed me how to take the cows out to pasture. Since every grazing area was rather small, cows could not roam freely but had to be tied on a long chain and after a while be relocated to another spot. He then tied the four cows together and took me to the pasture and told me to stay there until 7 PM In the meantime a strong thunderstorm came over the forest to the pasture. I tried to tie the cows together and go home but forgot how he did it. It rained buckets, and thunder crashed all around me. I was not successful trying to get the cows together. After a while, here came Johann in the rain and got me home. What a long day it was for me! In time I learned the trick of tying the cows together!

My primary reason for going to the Gerhards' was to have a change of scenery and better nutrition. The family was extremely hospitable and loving, unlike what I experienced at home. It took no time to assimilate with everyone in the family. The whole atmosphere was something I never experienced before. The family was so loving! Since they could not have children of their own, I became like a son to them. The food was terrific! For breakfast, after I cleaned the stalls, practically every morning we had eggs and bacon, home fries, and milk, and there was always plenty of everything. Their farm was strictly a family operation with less than forty acres. That included pasture and fields. They planted wheat, rye, potatoes, and sugar beets. For working the fields they used the two oxen. Since all the fields were on hillsides, and not one was on straight ground, the oxen were better suited than horses to work those fields. They had no tractor or heavy farm machinery. What could not be worked with the animals was done by hand. After less than two weeks they bought me some shoes that were more appropriate for the work I did, and I was so proud of them. My whole life somehow changed. The love and respect each one had for the other was unknown to me. There was no fighting going on, which was different than in our house. After four weeks I went home for a few days because they had a church festival/carnival in Ernst, and I wanted to be there. I came back to Mannebach after four days. The trip home took only two and a half hours since most was downhill! When I returned it took seven hours this time since I didn't get lost. I stayed with the Gerhards' family a total of thirteen weeks. Those weeks went by so fast I could hardly believe they were over. I learned a lot in those weeks, mostly harmony in the family, love for animals and the soil, and growing things. At the end of my time there I gained a total of thirteen pounds, felt physically and emotionally better, and gained a great love for agriculture and animals. Besides the shoes they bought me, they also gave me $40 when I left! I thought that was a lot of money! I left with a heavy heart knowing that things probably hadn't improved at home very much, and my hunch was right.

It was now the end of September when I got home. Not even three weeks had passed when my father came home on a nice afternoon after having talked to our minister about me. Since I did well in my confirmation assignments, they considered what direction I should take for my life. It was after lunch when father told me what the minister said to him: I should go into the ministry and devote my life for God's service. He also told me how my mother wished then already that if they ever had a son, he would be a pastor. But I told

78

father that I really felt that this was not my calling and that I would rather learn something that was more technical. I remember it as if it was today: he got up from his chair, came to where I was sitting, and beat me up badly for refusing him and the advice the pastor gave him. He would have this terrible sudden temper. This was now the second time that year that he beat me up. I knew that this would not be the last time. Exactly two weeks later, he came home for lunch after having talked to someone at the farm bureau who thought that I would make a good farmer and that I should learn the trade of farming. This time I just sat quietly and said nothing. He asked me if that was what I would like to do. I simply said that I would like something more technical for an occupation. He didn't like that. He got up again, but this time stepmother got up too and intervened on my behalf. Had she not done it, I don't know if I would be still alive today.

I don't know what caused his many mood swings. Perhaps it was the war years that got the best of him. One incident I can remember very well is when his pet dachshund got killed. His name was Hexie. He was a quiet little dog. Father brought him home in a little paper bag shortly after he was born. Mother had asked me to take the cow to graze along the Mosel River. I had to cross the highway, and the dog came with me. I was now on the other side, and little Hexie waddled behind me about a foot from the road's edge. A big semi-truck came at fairly high speed and drove right over the dog, killing him instantly. I returned home, carrying the lifeless dog. When mother saw me bring that dog home she beat me so hard that I could not stand on my own two feet. She never asked or inquired about the circumstance that killed the dog. It was pure brutality. But that was not all that day. When father came home and found out what happened, he too gave me a whipping that I never forgot. I am perfectly aware that there is a great attachment to an animal that is really strong. I always knew when the rules were broken there should be punishment. But this time I felt that I didn't deserve almost to be killed for something that was beyond my control.

So my memory of my home life is not what it should have been. What a contrast to the time spent with the Gerhards family, where I witnessed love and respect for everyone! I determined, even as a young man, that I would never treat my own children that way.

Chapter 9

On-the-Job Training

Have Thine own way, Lord. Have Thine own way.
Thou art the Potter, I am the clay.
Mold me and make me, after thy will.
While I am waiting, yielding and still.

Have Thine own way Lord. Have Thine own way.
Wounded and weary, help me, I pray.
Power, all power, surely is Thine.
Touch me and heal me Savior divine.

Adelaide A. Pollard (1907)

*A*s the rest of the year went on, my father sought a training farm for me where I would be in strict training for all aspects of farming. He signed a contract with a farm in Nastatten near Koenigstein in the Taunus Mountains, about forty kilometers from Frankfurt am Main, about 100 kilometers from home. The administrator of the farm was Mr. Scharenberg. He had a wife and two daughters. The farm belonged to a former cloister that also had a nursing home and a twenty-room hospital connected to it. Mr. Scharenberg was the administrator of that, too. It had about

140 acres of land that supplied the nursing home and the hospital with good wholesome food, all home grown. The farm had two Clydesdale horses, twenty cows, eight breeding pigs, and eighteen pigs for food.

I arrived on the farm New Year's Day 1952 for three years of training. Father just took me there without making any arrangements to see if the day was alright for me to come. Just as we arrived, the Scharenberg family was ready to leave for Frankfurt to see a play and do some visiting with friends. I sat all afternoon alone in their living quarters until 10:30 PM when they came home. Father just unloaded my suitcase and my bike and took off, never giving me a penny or anything (even a hug and a "goodbye" would have been nice). The contract stated that I would eat with the family, do minor tasks in the house, like stocking the furnace and cleaning their shoes, but my sleeping quarters were to be in an adjacent house on the farm. After about three months in Nastatten, my father wrote Mr. Scharenberg saying that I had never written a letter home and that Mr. Scharenberg should discipline me. Well, I told Mr. Scharenberg that I had no money for postage. All I had at that time was 20 cents to my name, and to mail a letter was 22 cents. I told him that my father had left me without any money. Mr. Scharenberg wrote father a nasty letter, and that solved that! He never wrote again!

The next day Mr. Scharenberg showed me all the details of the farm and my responsibilities of work both practically and theoretically. My first year had an emphasis on horses: their grooming, learning to work with them, and breeding. All three years I was not allowed to drive the tractor but could only use horses. I had to plow with horses and bring the wagons home fully loaded, handling them going up or down by myself and using all kinds of implements used on the farm. The second year the emphasis was on cows. Here too I learned breeding, including artificial insemination, milking, feeding, and animal health. That year we bought the first milking machine in the area. However, as the trainee, I had to milk three cows by hand every day. After that I would help with the machine, which also was my first liquid for the day, squirting fresh milk directly into my mouth. We also had a centrifuge to separate the heavy cream to make butter for the nursing home and hospital. Everyone on this farm always had fresh food.

My day started at 5 AM and ended at 6 PM I had to be cleaned up by then to eat supper with the family. We worked that time Monday through Friday. Saturday and Sunday, after milking and feeding the animals, were usually free except when special work needed to be done, like a raining period. One Sunday a month I had completely off. My pay that first year was 5 DM or ($1.25 a month). However I didn't get that money in my hand. Mrs. Scharenberg had a hand in it also. I would get 1 DM per month or .25 cents for church offering each Sunday, one DM for a haircut per month, one DM for candy per month, about .50 cents for postage to write home and the rest she saved for work shoes. The wage increased by one DM per year.

Training was not just in the field of study but in every area of one's life. Discipline was the name of the game! Also in my second and third years, I was required to attend specialized or trade schooling for agriculture once a week. Here we learned ground cultivation, agricultural chemistry, soil erosion and conservation, animal husbandry, and many related subjects. Some subjects were hands-on training, at which time we actually went to the fields that belonged to the school.

In the third year the emphasis was on pigs. Since we had eight breeding pigs, I learned all stages of pig farming. We cross-bred certain varieties for quick weight gain from birth to market and were able to have pigs weigh about 225 to 250 pounds in about three to four months. Every week a certain group was weighed, and if the combined weight gain three to four pounds a day was not reached, then that pig was sold for a roaster to a butcher. Their food consisted of steamed potatoes and oatmeal, very little water, and not too big a pen. They could move freely but not run very much. The pigs we raised for our consumption had it better. We were not so concerned about these pigs gaining weight so quick. They would be allowed to spend the day outside and play in the mud. A little funny story of the boar we had: In the adjacent villages many family farmers had one or two pigs that they brought to our Mr. Pig for breeding. It was often so funny that a farmer let his in-heat pig loose and the pig came all by itself to our farm, and when the farmer finally arrived, all the business was already done. I remember several came at least three and four kilometers to our farm. I never called a pig stupid!

On the Sundays I was completely off I usually rode my bike to various places in the Taunus Mountains. It was not unusual that I rode 80 to 100 kilometers that day. I would visit practically all the towns and castles on the Rhein River from Koblenz to Bingen. I had a friend from school that would go with me most of the time on those days. I forget his name now, but we were like brothers. His parents had a family farm in Nastatten where they primarily raised chickens. They had incubators that would hold a thousand eggs, and on the day they would hatch, after twenty-one to twenty-three days, they would determine immediately which was male or female. My friend usually called me on the day because that selection had to be done in the first few minutes after they were born. We looked at a certain spot and would see which it was. If it was a male it would immediately be killed, because they didn't want to raise roosters but egg-laying hens. We were about ninety-eight percent correct in the selection of roosters. When we determined it was a rooster, we gave it a special twist, and the rooster was gone.

The three years in Nastatten were hard years. Labor was cheap for the owner but also rewarding for the participant. Not only did I learn the trade of farming, but I gained a lot of character as well. Whether it was cleaning the boss's shoes or participating in the birth of a calf, every detail of life and knowledge was engraved in us, and that is something no one could take from us. Even then I thought how rewarding that time really was. We just never had time to go to a dance or other activity, and we learned not to miss any of those things.

In the spring of 1955 I had to go before a district agriculture committee for our State Diploma. I remember how I dreaded that day. There were four experts plus the teacher from the trade school that examined us. We had six trainees that day from various farms in the district. Each one appeared before a member of that committee for a specific subject. It lasted all day. We were asked things like how to determine the age of a horse by looking at their teeth, or things about animal breeding, or agricultural chemistry. You name it. Each session was about forty minutes per subject. The grading was either pass or fail. I passed on all subjects. I now was an agriculture journeyman, one step away from a Master Farmer. I was now relieved from my contractual obligation at the farm, which was officially called Gutsverwaltung Kaiser Willhelm Heim, Nastatten im Taunus.

The day came that I had to say good bye to the Scharenbergs. They had not only been my trainers those three years and four months, but also my mentors. They became like parents to me. They instilled some very good ethics in me that remain to this day. They made me go to church every Sunday without exception right after the animals received their care. Both of them went with me. Their oldest daughter was away in training to learn home economics. The younger daughter, Jutta, was still at home. As we left for church,

Mrs. Scharenberg would give me the .25 cents which she saved from my meager pay for the offering. Just not having money in the pocket was also training and restrained me from buying anything foolish, which was not possible anyway with the little I received. Here again I was accepted in a family that had no strife in the home; at least I never saw it. The family was always together. They played games together, sat by a radio and listened to German comics, and did many things that a family would do. The day my father picked me up, Mrs. Scharenberg whispered in my ear and said, "I prayed every week for you." Little did I understand what she was saying because nothing of this sort was ever spoken to me before, but eight years later I would understand. (I will come to that later.)

Chapter 10

Ordering My Steps

The steps of a man are established by the LORD, when he delights in his way. Psalm 37:23

He leadeth me O blessed thought!
O words with heavenly comfort fraught!
Whate'er I do, where'er I be, still 'tis God's
hand that leadeth me.
He leadeth me, he leadeth me,
by his own hand he leadeth me.
His faithful follower I would be for by his hand he
leadeth me.

Joseph H. Gilmore (1862)

*I*t was now April 1955. I stayed home only two weeks before I started a new job as a journeyman farmer. At a farm located in Weissenturm, on the beautiful Rhein River about 150 kilometers from home. Right across the river was the city of Neuwied where most of the action was, and a ferry by the foot of our street took us over the river. The farm was located right about the center of town, surrounded by houses, which was sort of strange. Weissenturm was an industrial city and the center of Bims, the place where volcanic ash just about encircled the city. That ash was used to make cinder blocks for construction. Companies came from everywhere, surrounding the city to get this product. Our farm had about 120 acres, half of which were on top of Bims and the other half below the mined product. The difference of the ground was about twenty feet deep. However, the soil was good above and below and supported a variety of products. We grew rye, wheat, sugar beets, potatoes, and summer grains, like oats and barley. In fact, the ground was so good that we made money by the good harvests we had of all we grew. The owner was also certified to have trainees both on the farm and in the household for girls to study home economics. We had two journey men, one trainee and the farmer's eighteen-year-old son, besides two girls who worked inside the house. We had only six cows, a few pigs, and two horses. I opted to work with the horses because of my love for them when I was at my training. Heavy work was done with the tractor. In about September father mailed me a letter that came from America, from my Tante Helen in Cincinnati. In her barely readable German she asked me and my sister Gerda if we had a desire to immigrate to America. She told of her sister, my mother, and her children, and wondered what happened to them. Now she would like to do something for them. America! That was a dream that many of us had, and I was the proud man that received even an invitation to get there! I was so excited that I was almost beside myself! The owner (I forget his name), instead of being happy for me, became my worst enemy. In the next two months he made life so miserable for me that I barely could stand it. Quitting time was always 5 PM, but from that time forward he always found things for me to do late in the evening. I remember one evening he made me sort potatoes for size until 2 AM That day I gave him two weeks' notice and left him at the end of October. I later found out that he never paid into my retirement fund. Even though not all was desirable there, I did have some happy moments. All the guys knew what a deep sleeper I was. Nothing could wake me up. I always had two alarm clocks, one next to me and the other at the end of the bed in a big glass bowl to be extra loud so that when it rang, I had to get up to turn it off. Half the time I heard neither. I slept on the ground floor. So the fellows got my whole bed, with me in it sleeping, took it outside, and set it in the middle of the farm. I never woke up during the whole ordeal. They wanted to see when I would wake up. I opened my eyes when the sun came up. I was two hours late! Life might never be what we wish, but there are enough moments that make up for bad ones, and I tried to focus on those. Things were also better financially for me. I started out getting 125 DM per month. It doesn't seem a lot, but it was better than 7 DM at the end of training, plus I had my room and board. After three months he gave me 135 DM, so I thought I was really rich. Things started to get better in Germany in a lot of ways, and I felt good about my wages. I also started to loosen up a little and allowed myself to see a movie here and there and go out with the girls to a dance with another guy across the river to Neuwied. I left Weissenturm at the end of November and went home.

Once home I got really busy applying to the American consulate for a visa to come to America to look for another job. The first reply I got from the consulate was that I would have to appear several times at their headquarters in Frankurt. That would require finding a job not too far from there. Low and behold, I found employment at a farm in Koenigstein im Taunus, only thirty kilometers from my training farm and only twenty kilometers from Frankfurt. The farm's name was Rettershof, only four kilometers from Koenigstein, a dream come through (Some say, "dream come true," but I like "dream come through"!). Its buildings dated back to 1146 as a cloister, beautifully nestled in a valley surrounded by a wonderful forest of beech trees and pine. It was a big farm for German standards, had almost 500 acres, and was completely mechanized; only four people worked the whole farm. The owner not only had the farm but also a foreign language school with over sixty permanent students, a riding facility with fifteen horses only for Americans stationed in Germany, with English speaking instructors. Also they had a garden shop and greenhouses to raise beautiful flowers just for the farm and restaurant with two people doing nothing else but raising flowers. Besides they had a restaurant that served German delicacies and pastries mainly for Americans stationed there. The area was known for the many fruit varieties, especially apples. In the fall we made over 12,000 liters of apple wine, and people from all over came for just that. They drank it hot and cold with cinnamon. On Saturdays and Sundays, when the weather was nice, more than

91

500 cars came to visit the place. The owner, whose name was Herr von Richter, surely knew how to make money on everything he laid hands on. The man was then already eighty-three years old and his wife was only fifty-three. Every morning his servants would get a horse ready for him and his wife, and both rode at least two hours come rain or shine. When he came home, each day he would say, "Wunderbar" (wonderful). Once a week he would invite us guys to play cards with him. When we entered the room he would single out one of us and say, "You smoke the cigar tonight to make the manly atmosphere." He did not smoke; neither did any of us, but everything had to be just so.

As stated earlier, the farm was completely mechanized. No horses were used in the farm. To get everything going with machinery, we had a blacksmith shop where we either made repairs or alterations to equipment or invented new ways to make the job easier. Each man had the freedom to do it. We had three journeymen farmers and one master farmer. We had all the equipment necessary for the operation of the farm. This included two Massey-Ferguson tractors and one Mercedes versatile vehicle called "Unimog." It could do almost anything. The administrator never worked in the fields. We raised wheat, rye, oats, barley, sugar beets, potatoes, tomatoes, fruits, and corn for silage. We were known to have early potatoes, which we sold as early as June, because we pre-germinated them in dark rooms with growing lights. The planting was done the middle of January, and kept from freezing with an elaborate sprinkling system on cold nights. The farm had also forty milk cows that were taken care of by a couple, who would milk them at 5 AM and 5 PM and feed them nothing else. The milk was sold and delivered to area hotels, nursing homes, vacation hotels, and private organizations. Butter was made fresh daily for our own consumption and for retail. We also had a few pigs for house consumption and a thousand egg laying chickens, and another thousand were raised for the following year.

I really enjoyed working there. All my co-workers were about the same age as I; only two were older than me, and one of them was married. My pay was now a whopping 200 DM per month, not too bad at the time for farm personnel, plus I had room and board and all the amenities that go along with it. We worked daily from eight to five, Saturdays and Sundays off. If we got called to do anything else other than farming, we got paid extra. That included even working fifteen minutes longer than required on the daily schedule. I also received my driver's license while there. The test was very strict, because a license is for life, and it took a whole day. The morning session was theoretical. The afternoon session was practical, where we had to drive all around Frankfurt in real traffic situations. We also had access to a car for personal use, so we fellows went to Frankfurt or Wiesbaden for our entertainment on weekends and only paid for gas. In the foreign language school worked two young girls whom we invited to come along for a movie or dance. On one occasion we ate in Frankfurt and went to a show. My date was tired before 10 PM, so I brought her home, got a ladder to reach the second floor, woke the other girl up, and took her with me to join my friends back in Frankfurt. I was a real party animal!

During my nine months on Retterhof, I was required to go several times to the American consulate. It was easier for me to be there in person than to handle the process by mail. At that time in 1956 the Hungarian uprising took place, which was followed by the Russian invasion of that country. Not only did we have refugees from East Germany in the West, but now they also came from Hungary. In America, Congress debated how many of these refugees would be allowed to come to America. President Eisenhower signed a bill that would allow 100,000 to come to America. Since I had refugee status in Germany, I was included in that number. It was the last week in September 1956 that my sister Gerda and I were called to the American Embassy in Frankfurt to see whether we were among those who would get a visa. The room was packed. Every so often someone was called into another room for further instructions and then would wait again. By late in the afternoon we were called in again and told that we would get our visa; along with that there were papers to sign, and arrangement documents were given to us for the transport from Germany to America. No one can describe the excitement that came over us in that moment.

Chapter 11

On to America

Commit now all your griefs and ways into His hands;
To His sure truth and tender care,
who earth and heaven commands.
Who points the clouds their course,
whom winds and seas obey,
He shall direct your wandering feet,
He shall prepare your way.

Far, far above your thought His counsel shall appear,
When fully He the work has wrought and
caused your needless fear.
Leave to His sovereign will to choose and
to command,
With wonder filled, you then shall own how wise,
how strong His hand.

Paul Gerhadrt, *1653*

*G*oing to America was the dream of so many Europeans,
and I was one whose dream came through. Our departure
date was given to us; it was December 5, 1956. That gave us only a
few weeks to get ready. When I started this job, I had informed the
owner of my intention to go to America if I could get a visa and that

there could come a time when I would have to leave in a hurry. He was very understanding and let me leave in a week's time. I left the Rettershof on November 1, 1956 and came home.

Now the process began to require all kinds of last-minute official decisions. I had to go to local authorities to officially sign papers that I would now leave Germany permanently, leave my homeland for good, and sever all relations here and now. This became a real soul-searching decision for a nineteen-year-old. To leave one's place of birth, parents, and friends was challenging, and it would not take much to persuade me to change my mind. I remember a great fear overcame me at the many decisions I had to make. Questions came to mind: "Could I really do it?" "Was I foolish to leave behind what was really all I had known all my life so far?" The initial excitement wore off with the fear of the unknown. I could hardly go through our little village of Ernst without someone telling me good luck, while others gave me the impression I was a traitor to my homeland. One man I remember told me, "Willi, I am proud of you and keep your head up even when the neck is dirty." He also asked me what state I would go. I said, "Ohio." "Oh," he said. "Is that Oheeo?"

The last two weeks were just terrible. Hardly anyone spoke to each other. It was almost like a funeral was in progress. At the slightest thing, tears would roll just about everyone's face. On the Sunday before we left, my parents invited my uncle Fritz, father's brother, and family over and some relatives from mother's side, namely her sister. Mother baked lots of good cakes and other goodies. Uncle

Fritz was always good at giving speeches, and this occasion was no different. He reminded me that no good German would leave his Fatherland forever, but I should remember, whatever length I stayed in America, never to forget where I came from and make it top priority to come home once I tasted the New World. All this started to have an effect on me. Should I really leave my home even though it was not often home to me?

Another concern I had was what to do with my dog. His name was Rolph. He, too, started to feel sorry about my leaving. He refused to eat his food. He was a mix of German shepherd and Dobermann, a truly unusual animal. I remember when we bought him from some Gypsies that came to town. Europe has a lot of Gypsies that travel from town to town, staying always a few days, sometimes even weeks. I remember the evening we bought him. Father and I went one evening after supper to a garden we had right next to the Mosel River. Here the Gypsies had parked next to our property. The man came out of his trailer and asked for money; not only that, but he told us that his wife was very sick and had no money to take her to the doctor. Father told him that he no money on him but would go home and bring some bottles of wine he could trade for money. We walked home and got seven bottles of wine and bought the dog. He was a seven-month-old and was trained in all kinds of tricks by the Gypsies: he would catch live rabbits and bring them right to you without killing them as well as small deer. He was unusually strong. He would never bark after he chased an animal, and very seldom did an animal get away from him. Rolph also loved our cat. She would always sleep with him in the doghouse, and they even ate food out of the same dish. Sometimes Rolph would carry her in his mouth, and the cat never made a peep.

They were just great animals. Rolph was naturally a great watch dog. He was not a great barker and would not touch anyone that came at night, but watch out when someone touched an item. He would bite right in the upper arm. All the people in town knew, "Watch out for Schakat dog." Enjoy everything you see, but don't touch.

The day of our departure, Monday, December 3, 1956, came. We left early in the afternoon by train to Bremen in North Germany. That morning was just terrible. No one spoke a word, and if they did, tears usually followed. In my case excitement overruled sadness. This was now another chapter in my life. My ways were now in the hand of God, and I left my family there. At the railroad station we exchanged the final good-byes. Father was extremely quiet. Mother, however, hugged us and gave each of us five German Marks. It was not much, but it came from her heart. It at least showed that she loved and cared for us. That was all she had, but father gave us nothing at all. That was perhaps the hardest thing to overcome. Nothing!

It took almost eight hours from Cochem to Bremen. I remember it was 10 PM when we arrived and we went to a hotel for the night. I only had a suitcase and Gerda had a small trunk. The next morning we went by bus to Bremerhafen where the ocean sailing vessels were. It's about a seventy-kilometer trip from Bremen to Bremerhafen.

There was a big building, and in the hall next to it was the place where all the passengers from all over Europe met. We would leave on the ship the next day. Here we had an orientation of all that would transpire on the trip. It was a big place; we ate there and also stayed overnight. After a late breakfast they started to take us by bus to the pier. There again was some shelter where we stayed a few hours until we could board the ship. The weather was a little misty, along with a light fog that sort of made it appropriate for saying good-bye to the homeland. On that section of the pier were three ships. I forgot the name of the first one, the second one was our ship, the *General Langfit*, and behind ours was at the time the world largest and fastest steam ship, the *United States*. I had read so much about it and took a walk alongside it. It was just amazing, and it would cross the ocean from Bremerhafen to New York in three days and ten hours.

Our departure time was slated for some time in the afternoon around 4 PM, but the time came and went, and we were still sitting there. The only ship leaving at 4 PM was the *United States*. I watched with excitement how they pushed that big ship into the channel for ocean crossing. Our ship was still sitting there with no thought of leaving. In fact they served our first meal aboard the ship at about 6 PM, and I thought we would take off soon afterward, but nothing happened. In fact, at about bed time we were still sitting at the pier. So I never found out when we actually left Germany, but later someone told me that it was 11 PM. I don't know why it was so late, but my only thought on this is that there were many people watching the departure, and the "good-byes" were easier at night because we were sleeping. However the next morning after I got up we were already cruising in the North Sea with no land in sight. That was an eerie feeling. Our ship had a cruising speed of 17 knots, about 27 mph, and the total time for arrival in New York was between nine to ten days if all was well.

The next day after breakfast came an announcement that anyone was willing to work and help with kitchen duties could apply for a job, about four to five hours a day and the great pay of $ 3.00 per day. I rushed to the place they told us to come and was hired. I needed the money badly since after I exchanged and paid all my expenses in Germany, I had a total of seven dollars to my name, not a lot of cash to make a trip to America. My ocean crossing and land transportation in America were paid for by the Lutheran

World Federation, an organization that provided the needed funds for refugees to come to America, which we agreed to repay within one year of arrival. They handed me a white apron and a cook's hat, and I was in business for duty. My first duty was lunch time in the kitchen and dining area for women and small children on the upper deck. I learned later that the upper deck at the center of the ship was the best place to be once it stormed. Also, they assigned me a crew member cook who made sure that I did the job right. He was a very fine man who befriended me right away. One thing peculiar about him was that he was a black man. When I grew up in Germany I never got to see a black person! In fact, the only one I ever saw was when a circus came to town and they had a little tent next to the main tent where they had a black man as an exhibit. We paid 25 cents extra to see him and shook hands with him. Now I had my own personal black friend, and for me it was an extreme privilege to have. We two hit it right off! I just couldn't get over that I had such an instant friend. Right away he taught me my first English, like "please pass the potatoes," "fill up the soup," "turn the eggs over," and simple things like that. It was exciting to learn, and he had such patience with me. This black man really made an impression on me. He also took a personal interest in me, like when he told me that after three days we would be through the English Channel and headed out into the Gulf of Biscayne. The open ocean, from the waves and storm, would be rougher then at present. He encouraged me not to get seasick so that I would not lose my job and pay. He gave me a tip: when waking up in the morning I should bite into some food that was ready to be eaten. So he gave me a cooked chicken leg before I went to sleep, and I had to bite into it in the morning before I had a second thought about anything, including food. I followed his advice, and sure enough, I never got seasick even though, as he said, the sea got rough and the waves high. In fact, on the fourth day as we entered the Gulf of Biscayne we hit a storm that lasted almost five days with high winds and waves between thirty and forty feet high. I was working in the upper dining room and the waves where higher than the ship. The first night of the storm, I woke up after a huge wave hit the ship so hard that I thought we hit an iceberg. My sleeping quarters were in the bow of the ship, and every wave knocked the ship from right to left and up and down, and then it would dive so far over the waves that the propellers got out of the water, and the ship would rattle like a tin can. This went on for the duration of almost five days.

Naturally during the storm, fewer and fewer people came to get food. In fact, one day we counted the people that came to the cafeteria, and we had only three hundred people out of over two thousand, but every day they cooked as if two thousand came to eat. I, coming out of war-torn Germany could hardly bear the waste, but whatever was not eaten was thrown overboard, and the sea gulls that followed the ship in Bremerhafen were also there when we finally got to New York.

I did not have any previous experience in ocean travel, so not seeing land was tremendously exciting for me. The people responsible for bringing us to the New World had daily programs going that would inform us of the many facets of American life. In fact, on the eighth of December, 1956, they published an onboard newspaper called *Die Einwanderer Post*, the *Immigrant Post*. They also had a shop where one could buy a few small things. Some items, like a chocolate bar, were only .05 cents. I only looked since I only had a few dollars and did not know if in an emergency I might need those five cents! Not everyone was a refugee, and some could afford the items. There were some things that I learned from these travelers. One was the superstition of Friday the 13th. This day was said by many to be a very "bad luck" day. I was told never to start a job on a Friday.

Also, American coins and paper money were introduced to us along with the value of each coin. Another thing they made us aware of was American songs from Native American and Negro Spirituals. This type of music was new to me. We learned one song that stuck somehow in my mind.

1. *When Israel was in Egypt's land; let my people go,*
   Oppressed so hard; they could not stand, let my people go.
2. *Go down Moses; way down in Egypt's land*
   Tell ole Pharaoh, let my people go
3. *Thus spoke the Lord, bold Moses said: let my people go,*

If not I smite your firstborn dead; let my people go.
4. *No more shall they in bondage toil; let my people go,*
   Let them come out with Egypt's spoil, let my people go.

I thought this little spiritual song fit me right to a *T*!

Mornings and afternoons on the ship they had English classes for beginners and those that were more advanced. So I got some of my English lessons from my cook friend who taught me a little every day. They also would show us movies about America and other cinemas. One of the daily programs was, *Das Leben in den Vereinigten Staten* which means *Life in the United States*. Here we learned about the average daily life of Americans, which I thought was very interesting. In the evening they had a band playing and dancing. This I liked a lot. Dancing, however, was not the easiest thing to do when the ship rolled and gyrated through the heavy sea. Nevertheless, I had fun. Here onboard the ship were many different ethnic groups that displayed their talents and customs. Most of their ethnic clothing was packed away; nevertheless I had a ball doing all that different stuff. Also along with Germans, Hungarians, Rumanians, Turks, Italians, Yugoslavians, and who knows what other nationalities, the Hungarians formed an all-male choir. Since we were now approaching Christmas, they would sing their native Christmas carols along with other native music. I was intrigued by the harmony of these men. I sat some days for hours just to listening to them. Everyone who at any time listened to an all-male choir can attest to how beautiful such a choir sounds. I observed how quickly these people formed some leadership among themselves. It seemed like out of nowhere some stood up and guided this group or that. It was just a wonderful blend of people, and I was amazed at how those coming from many backgrounds and cultures could in some way form such beautiful harmony.

Had everything gone as planned we could have been in New York in two more days, but the trip was extended now to thirteen days. However the next couple of days were rather nice. The sun shone on most days, and it was rather pleasant to sit on deck. The average weather and sea water temperature was now about 56 F. Naturally, this was no cruise ship; nevertheless, they had lounge chairs and other means to sit and walk on board. Since the ship was over 480 feet long, one could take quite a stroll on it. The bow naturally always had some head wind while the stern area was nice and still. When I was off my duties in the kitchen, I would spend most of my free time outside. Even though it was sunny, one would just about always use a jacket. It was December, after all! I also made some good friends on board. Their names I have forgotten, but we had a good acquaintance. One was a young lady named Barbara Mateyka. She came always to the dances. The other fellow was my age, whose name I forgot, but he went to the city of Findley, Ohio. Barbara went to Coquille, Oregon. She had a train ride of several days after leaving New York. We kept in touch many years afterward; however, Barbara went to college in Eugene, Oregon, and the one from Findley got drafted into the U.S. Army about seven months later. He was sent back to Europe, mainly France, and I lost contact with him.

Slowly but surely we got out of the heavy storm. On some days we traveled only barely 200 sea miles in a twenty-four-hour period. Now the weather got better, and on December 17, 1956, we were only 900 hundred miles from New York. The next few days were just beautiful. The ocean was smooth, and we traveled 390 miles in a twenty-four-hour period. That was just great! On December 19, we headed into a storm that came from the continent for about six hours. No land was yet in sight, but the storm was so strong on the port side that the ship listed almost 15 degrees steady from early afternoon until evening. Not knowing a lot of sea behavior, I found it strange that a ship of this size did not right itself, but they told us not to worry about anything. My excitement grew by the minute. I could hardly contain myself, always thinking about what would be the first thing I would see in America. Two more times I was required to do my duty in the dining room, this evening and the next morning, the twentieth. After my kitchen duty I went on deck until late in the evening. I remember looking ahead, and low and behold, I saw in the far distance the first lights as we approached Long Island, New York. I tried to stay up for a while, but a crew member told me to go to bed, because I would not see very much anyhow. The next day would be an extremely hard day. Besides, the ship would drop anchor before getting too close into New York harbor.

My kitchen duties were from 7:30 to 9:30 the next morning, half an hour later than usual. This allowed the passengers more time to eat and feel better because after going on land they had to provide for themselves. However, I got up at five in the morning. I stood alone in the bow of the ship and watched how the tug boats came along the ship and slowly pushed it into New York harbor. It was a great excitement for me but also a great emotional strain at that moment. I cannot really describe it, but I was overcome with an exceptionally great fear and loneliness that I would somehow be lost in this great country. The New York skyline, the tall buildings, the traffic along Henry Hudson Parkway, were all just too much at the moment, so early in the morning. It was just overwhelming to me. I knew in a little while I had to go to the kitchen, but the sight of all that took place at that moment was just overwhelming at that time. I didn't know it at the time, but God gave me an assurance that I never felt in my life. I think that for the first time in my life I uttered a prayer from my very heart. The words came very spontaneously to me: "Lord, don't let me get lost in this great country." Right after this it seemed that all fears and unknowns were gone! Never before had I found so quick a relief of something that bothered me and never before could I believe that God heard a prayer from someone who was everything but a child of His. All the head knowledge from my confirmation came into focus. Am I heading to some home that is unknown to me? These were some precious hours I had alone in the bow of the *General Langfitt* the morning of December 20, 1956.

I left my hallowed place and went to my station in the kitchen. The cafeteria was unusually full as well as the dining area for women and children where I worked most of the time. It looked like everyone was hungry, and most knew that this meal had to hold for them several hours before they would get another meal. It was every man for himself after that. During the breakfast hours several announcements came to guide the people how they should leave the ship. In the meantime the ship was pushed to Pier #86. The second announcement called for the procedure of disembarking that was done alphabetically. After 10 AM people with their proper name could proceed to leave the ship and go to their proper customs station where their belongings would also be found alphabetically. It was a slow procedure. Those of us who worked had a lot of work to do. All dishes, pots and pans, and implements for cooking had to be carefully washed and even steamed for sanitary reasons. The whole place was washed and cleaned to perfection, even the floors and tables. Also all the chairs that were tightened to the floor during the storm had to be loosed and properly stored.

The captain then sent the following declaration to all the ones that contributed to the safe journey:

> *As the end of the voyage approaches, it is my desire*
> *on behalf of the Master and the crew, members of*
> *the Military Department, ICEM and Trip Staffs, to*
> *express our sincere appreciation to all passengers*

aboard for the cooperation received in making this a safe and pleasant voyage. It is our earnest hope and desire that the inconvenience and restriction inherent in a voyage by sea will be outweighed by the friendships established, and pleasant memories encountered. Our particular thanks is extended to The passengers that performed duties in the cafeteria, dining rooms, and cleaning details. It is very apparent that you have all done your best to keep the U.S.N.S LANGFITT, in a clean and sanitary condition. We also like to thank the compartment leaders, those, who in such an able manner, assisted the TRIP staff in it's organizational and recreational activities, and the innumerable others, who served voluntarily to make this voyage a success.

Our best wishes go with you as you leave for your new homes in the United States. Until we meet again, thanks for your splendid cooperation and spirit, and the very best of luck.

Signed H.V. McClimon

LCDR. US Navy

Commanding Officer Military Department

I was very proud of myself that I also had a part in the safe and often pleasurable voyage.

Chapter 12

The Beginning of a New Life

Therefore, if anyone is in Christ, he is a new creation.
The old has passed away; behold the new has come.
2 Corinthians 5:17

I am Thine, O Lord, I have heard Thy voice,
and it told thy love to me.
But I long to rise in the arms of faith and
be closer drawn to Thee.

> Draw me nearer, nearer blessed Lord,
> to the cross where Thou hast died.
> Draw me nearer, nearer, nearer blessed Lord,
> to Thy precious bleeding side.

There are depths of love that I cannot know
till I cross the narrow sea.
There are heights of joy that I may not reach
till I rest in peace with Thee.

Fanny J. Crosby (1875)

After all that needed to be done for me it was almost
11:30 AM. Now came the great moment when those
who worked would get their great pay. I got $39 for my thirteen days

of work at sea. I felt like a millionaire! During the trip I practically spent nothing, just clinging to my $7!

12:30 came, and they announced that those whose last name began with the letter *S* could prepare to leave the ship. Lots of *S* people lined up the gangplank to the pier. My sister Gerda and I waited anxiously to step on shore. If my recollection still serves me right, it was 1:10 PM that day that I finally stepped on American soil on Pier 86 in New York City. No one came to greet us, no band was playing, and actually not much commotion was on the dock area. I suppose some passengers had family or friends come to greet them, but relatively very few. Probably most went to other states and did not stay in the New York area. We went to Ohio and some, like Barbara, went to Oregon.

The first person that approached us however, was a fine young black man, a representative from the Lutheran World Federation. The reason I say he was a fine man is because he was very well dressed and spoke fluent German to us. He greeted us in the name of the World Federation and welcomed us to New York and America. He helped us get through customs and took us to a waiting bus that would take us to Grand Central Railroad Station. He was one of several people from the federation that helped people find their way. He was now the second black person I had come in close contact with, and I was very impressed with his demeanor. I started to have a special love for that race.

The distance from the pier to the station was not far, and it only took a short time. He then took us to the place where we would wait for the train to Cincinnati at 5:30 PM and left to help others. Grand Central is a great place. Thousands of people come and go almost at the same time. Everything around me was great, just like America. While waiting for the train's arrival, I ventured to get a little taste of my new surroundings and tried to buy two hot dogs. I saw the sign, "hot dog 15 cents." So I thought if I gave the man 30 cents, he would give me two hot dogs. Well, he said a lot of things I could not understand, and in the end I got one hot dog, and he got the rest of my money. There was a tax on the hot dogs, so 30 cents was not enough, and the man wanted additional money. I learned quickly that understanding a language is very important. I came back with some more money and bought Gerda her hot dog. It was, however, a nice big hot dog with ketchup on it, which I had never tasted before.

Our train arrived at 5 PM with a 5:30 departure. Another first for me was that they pushed the last car in first. I had never seen that. The train was rather long because it had a long way to go and made stops in Trenton, New Jersey; Harrisburg, Pennsylvania; Pittsburgh, Pennsylvania; Columbus, Ohio; and Cincinnati, Ohio. These are the only stations I remember, but perhaps there were more. I'm sure that at some point I must have slept a while on the sixteen-hour trip. A couple of new experiences took place in the first few hours in America. As we boarded the train people noticed almost instantly that we were foreigners. Quite a few came and greeted us and said a lot of things we had trouble understanding, but some things we did. One couple a few seats forward gave Gerda and me an orange, which I thought was great since I hardly ever got one at home. Then at about 9 PM, another couple brought each of us a pillow for the night. I thought this was incredible, too, since we were strangers and these people extended such a warm welcome to us. Then at about two in the morning someone tapped me on the shoulder and invited me to the dining car to have a beer. That word beer I understood since the pronunciation in German is the same as in English, but the spelling is different, Bier. He ordered two beers and got the conversation going. Then he ordered another beer for himself. After that he said, "Excuse me for a moment," but never returned, and I had to pay $4 for the beer. So I learned rather quickly that even in America there will be good and not so good people around. I felt bad; first I hardly ever had a beer to drink, especially not at two in the morning, plus I lost $4. The rest of the trip was rather uneventful, except to note how big the country was. One can travel almost seventeen hours and only see a third of the country. What must the rest be? I thought about Barbara, who had to go a few days longer, to Oregon.

We arrived in Cincinnati about 10:30 AM. It was a beautiful, sunny day for December. Uncle Bernard and Tante Ottilie came to the train station to pick us up. We immediately marveled at the beautiful murals that were displayed in the station about the pioneering life and industrialization in Ohio and in Cincinnati in particular. Uncle Bernard had a one-year-old car, a 1955 Oldsmobile;

I could hardly imagine such big automobile. Also, it had no clutch; it was automatic. I was initially scared, because I thought, "How is he going to stop this thing?" As it turned out, it was rather smooth. I just had never seen a car with an automatic transmission. On the way home, they took us through downtown and many of the sites in Cincinnati. They lived in North Side, on 4265 Chambers St. At that time it was a quiet neighborhood. That house had seen a lot of activity after the war. We too had received many care packages from this place. Tante Ottilie had the whole family involved to gather items together for us needy ones in Germany.

It was now Friday, December 21, 1956, only four days before Christmas. Tante Ottilie took us to a department store, Shillitos, the next day and bought us something American: a pair of jeans and a flannel shirt. The excitement of arriving in the New World overshadowed any thought of Christmas being away from home. I myself was not homesick in any way but enjoyed every minute with my newfound cousins. On Christmas Day we were all together: there was Uncle Bernard, Tante Ottilie, Marion, Peggy, and John; my cousins; Ralph, Marion's husband; Edward Knoll and wife Vera; Gerda; and me.

Tante Ottilie prepared a big turkey for dinner with all the usual American trimmings. This was another first for me. In Germany we ate a goose for Christmas. This was different, however, but I remember it was just great.

Ed Knoll and his wife, Vera, lived in Metamora, Michigan. Ed, my cousin, was the son of my Tante Ida who immigrated to the United States sometime in 1921, along with Tante Ottilie and Tante Selma. My father had instructed Uncle Bernard on his visit to Germany that if and when I came to America to secure a job for me to work in my learned profession. Also, as my sponsor, he was obligated to find employment for me. True to his promise, he engaged Ed Knoll to find me a job in Michigan on a farm, and Ed came down over the holidays to pick me up. Talking over the prospect of going to Michigan so soon after my arrival scared the best of me. Not knowing the language and customs and being away so far from Cincinnati frightened me. So I did not go with him. Uncle Bernard was not too happy with my decision but understood my concerns and did all he could to alleviate my fears in my new environment. I stayed with the Biedenkapp's less than two months after my arrival. After that I moved in with my other Tante Irene and Uncle Adolf Tiepel. Uncle Adolf was a brother of my mother and had come to the United States in 1952. He had bought a house already that was only a few blocks away from the Biedenkapp's. So the move was agreed upon by all concerned. I lived with Tante Irene and Uncle Adolf about two and a half years. The Tiepels had two children, Edith and Erick. They were my true cousins. Both went to school, Edith in high school and Erick in grade school. I enjoyed my stay, especially Tante Irene's cooking. I am grateful to all of them to this day!

During and after the holidays a couple of interesting things happened. I wanted to notify all my friends in Germany first of my safe arrival in America and second of my job search. After Christmas I bought some post cards of Cincinnati, addressed them, and went to the post office in the Northside section of Cincinnati. While purchasing the stamps at the counter, I overheard two people behind me speaking in German. I turned around and introduced myself to them and told my name. The lady was about forty-five years old, and her son was nineteen. Her name was Maria Lange, and her son was Herbert. When I told them my name was Schakat, it immediately struck a nerve, and they asked what my mother's name was. I told her, "Stephanie." She turned around for a moment and sort of regained her composure and told me that she knew my mother! In fact, they were best friends as children, and besides she attended my parents' wedding in Lithuania! One cannot imagine the shock as I was in hearing all of this. Coming halfway around the world and finding someone who knew my parents! Besides, Maria told me that when my parents got married, my father ran out of wine during the celebration. She secured one shoe from every guest. The guest then had to buy back his or her shoe, and with the proceeds she bought some more wine to celebrate three additional days!

Earlier in this story I made mention that my grandmother, mother's mother, had flown in 1948 to America. Now I learned that Maria Lange had brought grandma out of Lithuania when they, as we, fled from the advancing Russian army, which at that time had killed her husband in front of her five children. She and my Tante Irene got a wagon with two horses, fled their home, and brought her eventually to a refugee camp in Germany. The Lange family became an important source of information to me. Mrs. Lange told me everything I wanted to know about my mother,. It was from her I learned every detail of my mother's life, her personality, and her person in general. She told me that she was a happy person, would sing most of the day, enjoyed all of her children, and made all of the clothes for them. She also told me about her over two-year fight with cancer and of her untimely death in 1941 when I was three years and ten months old.

Just a side note here on the blessing of meeting Maria Lange and what she told me of my mother: My mother's hometown in Lithuania was Siluva, and as a teenager she would visit Maria Lange (her married name) who lived in Raseiniai about eight kilometers from her house. Every summer one of the girls went to see the other. I don't know how they became good friends, but they did spend much time together. My grandfather and grandmother on my mother's side lived in Siluva. My grandfather had a blacksmith shop in town. He was a well-respected blacksmith in town. He was even asked to build the iron fence around the cemetery there but was told him that since he was not Roman Catholic, he could not be buried there. During World War II, Germans that lived in Lithuania were persecuted along with Germans that lived in East Prussia. The Lange family was a target, too. They caught Mr. Lange as he was riding his bicycle and took him in front of his family and shot him dead. Mrs. Lange was pregnant with her fourth child at the time. The family moved to Anerusum, a few villages from Raseiniai. When the time came for them to leave their homeland because of the Russians, they remembered my grandma who lived in Siluva. My grandpa must have already been dead. Herbert, now my best friend in America, built a sled and put my grandma and all the kids in it, with feed for the horses, and left Lithuania. He pulled it over 100 miles! This occurred about the same time we left our village. I did not know anything of what happened with my grandpa or grandma. They experienced the same cold weather we did, but instead of ending up in Denmark, like us, they ended up in a German refugee camp in Geldorf, Germany. In the meantime, as providence would have it, my mother's brothers and sisters in America looked for their mother (my grandmother) and found her with the Lange family in Geldorf. That is when they brought her to America at the age of seventy-seven. She was so weak that she needed several units of blood to strengthen her for the trip.

The second thing was finding a job. Herbert Lange and I became ready friends. Our occupations in Germany did not lend themselves to finding appropriate employment here. Herbert was a bricklayer, and I was a professional farmer. Also the timing after the holidays was not good for finding a job. So for the next three weeks Herbert and I went every day from factory to factory trying to locate a job. Now my other Tante Helen, then about sixty-eight years old, got into the act. She had a great conviction that God is in control of everything in our lives, and she went along one day.

One day she targeted the Cincinnati Milling Machine Co. Early that day we took the bus as usual and got there when the employment office opened at nine. We signed in along with at least twenty other people looking for a job. During the day they would interview one after another, and nothing happened to us. Then at about 2 PM, my aunt went to the man in charge behind the desk and literally cried to the man and told him these young men came from Germany and needed a job badly. Then she told him that when she was a young nurse, she took care of the founder of the Milling Machine Co. and that these boys need to be hired! Simply faith in action! I don't know if something like this ever came before this man, but the result was that both of us got hired that day and to my recollection, no one else did. As God says, "My ways are not your ways."

We started immediately. Both of us had a physical that took about an hour, and then we were introduced to the person we would work with for the first six weeks of learning English measurements, Herbert on a milling machine and I on a lathe. That whole process took about three hours while Tante Helen sat in the waiting lounge. The following day we reported to our respective places, Herbert in department 12–1, I in department 12–2, at seven in the morning. The man assigned to me was Ernest Danker, of German descent, who still spoke fluent German.

For the next six weeks I learned everything that was to be learned to work on the lathe, including the use of a micronometer and other measurement tools. After the six weeks I was to work the second or night shift, starting at 5 PM. We worked eight- or ten-hour shifts, depending what needed to be done. Our department was producing spare and specialized parts and, if time permitted, other items. Also, I acquainted myself with the method of working with unit hours. Every piece we made had a time attached to it so in an eight-hour shift we could produce 480 unit hrs. Every week, the performance of everyone in the department was posted on the bulletin board for all to see, and if we produced over 480 unit hours per day, we would get paid a bonus.

I enjoyed working at the "Mill" as it was called. Two more Germans came to work a few weeks after I started; they were Mr. Gessner and his son Horst Gessner. Both worked with Herbert in department 12–1. We all became friends right away, since the Gessners came from Berlin, and we had lunch together every day. Not too long after this, Mr. Gessner was transferred to the day shift, so Horst and I started to drive together to work the night shift. Horst bought himself a '54 Buick and I and sister Gerda bought a '53 Mercury. However the dual ownership didn't work out too well, so I bought myself a '54 VW. We alternated driving every week to go to work. We both enjoyed working the night shift and after working either eight or ten hours, we stopped every morning at the White Castle at Reading and William Howard Taft Road. We had just about the same items every day and stayed there until five or six in the morning and went to bed.

The year was now 1957 and as was the custom of the "Mill," they closed the plant for two weeks for vacation. So we Germans made some plans. Herbert Lange, Horst Gessner, and I planned a trip to the east part of the country along with another German, Helmut Wolfsberger. We four took Horst's '54 Buick and traveled through Pennsylvania, New Jersey, New York City, Connecticut, Massachusetts, back to New York State, Niagara Falls, Ontario, back along Lake Erie and then back home. We had a great time visiting the eastern part of this great country. We had no tent, slept on air mattresses and when it rained, in the car, really roughing it. We had a lot of joy seeing the eastern part of our new-found land.

Earlier, I mentioned a prayer I said on the bow of our ship, the *General Langfit*, early the morning as we were pushed into the harbor on Pier #86: "Lord, don't let me get lost in this great country." As I look back on this time, I now know that God was working all these years to bring me to Himself. No creature deserves anything. All that we receive comes from the goodness of God. Even those that never acknowledge the God of Scripture receive his common grace daily, for it is God that sustains them, feeds them, and gives them their every breath. Without His sovereign will to keep them alive they would die in a second! The Spirit of God was awakening my heart to see Him behind all of my life's circumstances. Even though at this point I was not trusting Christ as my Savior, He kept me alive through the war, got me to America, and provided a job, a wonderful family, and friends. Meeting the Lange family in that North Side post office was another work of His grace. Unbeknownst to me was the fact that Herbert became acquainted with the evangelical gospel before leaving Germany. God used his influence to introduce me to a living union and vital relationship with Jesus Christ.

Herbert had become my best friend. He asked me to attend a Bible study in his family's apartment on Chase Avenue in North Side. This was the time when God was awakening me to the truth of Christ. Pretty soon, we found other German youth who were interested in studying the Bible. In fact, we soon had between twenty-five and thirty Germans that came every Saturday evening for the study. Many worked as domestics in the city of Cincinnati. I had by then my first car, so I was able to bring all that wanted to come to the study. Not only did we study the Bible, but we also sang German folk songs that we learned in German and English. The Lange family consisted of five members: Mrs. Marie Lange, a widow; daughters Erna and Lilli; Herbert, Erika, and Roland. Herbert played the mandolin, Lilli and Erika both played guitar, and the rest sang.

The next two people that came into my life were two German deaconesses that worked in the inner city of Cincinnati. They looked like Catholic nuns, with long black dresses, a white head dress, and everything else black. Their names were Herta and Berta (German spelling). Herta was tall and outgoing. There was always a smile coming out of her headgear. Berta was more quiet, reserved, and introspective but also very sweet. Initially, I didn't know what brought them to Cincinnati, but I soon learned that they represented a German mission with headquarters in Schoolis Mountain, New Jersey. It was a German mission organization called The Liebenzell Mission in Germany. They worked in several churches, but primarily in the Concordia Lutheran Church on Race Street downtown. I also did not know what brought them over to our youth group, but I later learned that another German family, the Friederichs, knew them, and they were responsible for inviting these two to our group. Now we had some experts in our midst. They knew the Word of God well. They ordered German Bibles for us so we all had the same text of the Word of God. This German Bible was one of my most precious possessions. I loved it but still did not know the full meaning of it all.

These two sisters invited our group to the churches they ministered in to hear the Gospel and sing some German gospel songs, so the Lange girls and Herbert brought their guitars and mandolin along and sang on many different occasions. I, too, sang along with the beautiful lyrics, but the words did not make it into my inner being. Somehow they were foreign to me. It was not long until I did understand the new meaning. They spoke of salvation and commitment and surrender, which I knew I did not possess. I knew then that if I ever wanted to go to heaven, I had to make big changes in my life. Since I did not grow up in a Christian home, the learning was slow, and the spiritual vocabulary was missing. However, like everything else, and with God's help, one can do a lot of things that in the natural seem almost insurmountable.

Chapter 13

America the Beautiful

O Beautiful for spacious skies,
for amber waves of grain,
For purple mountain majesties above the fruited plain.

America, America, God shed His grace on thee,
And crown thy good, with brotherhood,
from sea to shining sea.

Katharine Lee Bates

*E*arly in the summer of 1958, my Uncle Arnold, my mother's uncle, living in California, invited me and my cousin Regina, who had come about six months after me to America, to visit him, and he would pay our way by train. I had now a job at the Cincinnati Milling Machine, and Regina worked as a domestic for some family. We made some plans to go, then my friend Horst Gessner from the "Mill" asked if he and his girlfriend Barbara could come with me. So we changed our plans and included those two. Uncle Arnold was satisfied with our decision. This trip was very exciting to us because while still in Germany, I read much about America, and this trip would highlight much of what I learned. I had bought in Germany a book entitled, *California Symphony*. Its English subtitle was *Jubilee Trails*. It traced the westward move of the American people after gold was found in California. It was then interesting reading, but now we had a chance to trace all the towns and cities mentioned in the book. So we left for California on the old highways and by-ways. In St. Louis we picked up the famous Route 66, which took us all the way to the Golden State. In 2008, I had the opportunity to retrace some of the old Route 66 we traveled on. It was then one of the few roads to the West. It was mostly a two-lane highway except for a stretch that was the "Will Rogers Expressway." I think it was one of the first experiments of building super highways. The immense greatness and beauty of this country overwhelmed us, and the people were so gracious and friendly, so open and helpful, with our still broken English. We traveled along this famous highway all the way to California through Texas, New Mexico, and Arizona. We visited Albuquerque and Santa Fe, all cities mentioned in the book. In Santa Fe, the owner of a restaurant, who noticed that we were Germans, welcomed us and made all the people dance and sing to the music of a band he had playing. We joined right along with them. We stopped at the Painted Desert and just took in the beauty of this whole country. The weather was unbearably hot, hotter than what we had in Germany. Daily the temperature was 100 degrees and above. But we decided to go through the desert in the daytime rather than at night as most people did. We got to Needles, the first town in California, at about ten in the morning, when the temperature was already 115 degrees. We stopped for gas and the owner told us, "If you guys want to travel this desert in daytime, I have to remove your thermostat from your engine." It was good advice for us German greenhorns, because the temperature climbed over 135 degrees inside the car while driving. I remember only one restaurant between Needles and San Bernardino. When we entered, a big fan cooled the place, but only to 98 degrees. I had ordered myself a cool milkshake and sat by the bar on some typical high chairs just as one sees in the Western movies. When Regina and Barbara came in from the outhouse, Regina took my cool drink and gulped it down without stopping. The next thing I knew, I saw Regina falling off the chair and lying half unconscious on the floor. The temperature difference was just too great between her body and the inside of the restaurant. I remember that the lady behind the counter saw it, got a pail of water and poured it on her, just as one sees in a Western movie. However, despite that, we all had a good time.

We finally arrived at our destination. Uncle Arnold lived in Wittier. He had a beautiful home and property with lots of fruit trees and in particular, avocadoes. He and his wife served many dishes with avocadoes in them, which was new to us. Uncle Arnold got a little older and did not feel good enough to drive us around, so every day he told us where to go. We took trips in the surrounding area, exploring cities and the countryside in the west. We visited

Hollywood with the, "Grumman Chinese Theater," Long Beach, which hosted the Miss America Pageant, Knott's Berry Farm, Disneyland—which had just opened that year—and the Laurence Welk show. In Hollywood we had an interesting experience at a local restaurant. We four sat in a famous eating place and didn't get served. People that came after us ate and left while we still sat there waiting for someone to serve us. Finally, I said to the others, "If I speak to the waitress in German maybe she will serve us." So I said to her in German, "Freulein, wollen sie uns nicht bedienen," which, translated, means, "Miss, why don't you serve us." Her response was, "Just one moment." This young woman understood German!

Uncle Arnold had also a brother who lived not far from him. His name was Alexander. He had three married daughters: Amilda, Natalia, and Ruth, and all three lived close to each other. We stayed a few nights with Natalia. All in all, we stayed in the area eight days. We left the Los Angeles area and drove the coastal road 1A to San Francisco. It was a scenic and beautiful trip. San Francisco is a beautiful city. We drove over the Golden Gate Bridge and through the Bay Tunnel. The Golden Gate Bridge was so exciting. From there we went to Sacramento and then to little State Route 88 to Nevada. Route 88 had just opened. It was now the end of July, and snow was still on the side of the road. We then drove to Reno, Nevada and from there to Salt Lake City. Here we went swimming in the Great Salt Lake. Swimming in the Salt Lake was an experience by itself. Even keeping one's feet in the water was a great challenge. As we were checking in the motel for the night, our two girls talked about the family that checked in next to us and, in German, they were talking about how cute the young man was and were guessing his age, thinking he could not understand German. The next morning they left just before us and when we met them later in the restaurant, he paid his bill and then came back to our table and said, "By the way, I'm twenty-five!" One never knows who understands another's language!

Denver was our next destination. The mountain passes before Denver were just beautiful. At 13,000 feet above sea level, our car just barely made it. Most people put wet rags over their carburetors to attract more oxygen to make it up the steep road. The motel owner gave all of us a large Mexican hat the next morning. It was all the way a beautiful, exciting, and educational trip. We had also planned to go to Yellowstone Park, but a car repair held us up for over a day, so we canceled it.

Chapter 14

Let There Be Light

In their case the god of this world has blinded the minds of the unbelievers, to keep them from seeing the light of the gospel of the glory of Christ, who is the image of God.

⁵ For what we proclaim is not ourselves, but Jesus Christ as Lord, with ourselves as your servants for Jesus' sake.

⁶ For God, who said, "Let light shine out of darkness," has shone in our hearts to give the light of the knowledge of the glory of God in the face of Jesus Christ. 2 Corinthians 4:4–6

*I*t was in the fall of 1958 that I had a serious car accident. As I was coming home from work after I worked all night, a drunk went through a red light and hit me head on in my little Volkswagen. The impact crushed the front end, knocked out the windshield, and left me with my head outside the car and my body inside the car. A police officer standing on the other side of the street witnessed the whole thing and took me to the hospital. It took twelve stitches to get my eyelids back on, and I had a gash on my right temple and numerous other abrasions. I stayed home for the next two days.

I know these things called, "accidents" happen every day, but they do not occur without God's design and purpose. God used this to awaken me to the brevity of life. While I was recuperating, lots of questions entered my thinking. First, I thought that life can be wiped out in a moment. Second, I questioned whether I prepared for the eternal. Third, I wondered what I could do about it. I realized that life is very fragile. We must give eternity our best thought, and I knew I had to aggressively change course. Even at my rather young age, about twenty-one now, I was concerned that I would spend the rest of my life having thoughts about eternity and God's personal love for me. Now was when God spoke, "Let there be light in Willi's heart." With a regenerated heart, now God granted repentance and faith. I knew God could do a much better job of leading my life than I could. This did not occur suddenly or some flash from heaven, but gradually. I felt that a burden had been lifted in my life that I could not carry alone. I related earlier that I purchased a German Bible for myself, and now I studied all the things that God required, not tradition or man-made laws. The Bible became my text book in all that I planned or did. This freed me from the cumbersome rules I was used to. Not that all changed immediately, but as time went on I began to see evidence of God's Spirit living in my heart. I could finally say that whatever happened to me now, I was prepared for eternity because of God's grace alone.

I have learned that believers are aliens and strangers in this world. As a refugee, I did not have a home. When I came to America I thought I had finally found a home to call my own. But the Bible says that, "This world is passing away, along with its lusts" (1 John 2:17). As John Bunyan pictured in his classic book, *Pilgrims Progress,* we are all born in the City of Destruction. This world is not a lasting kingdom! The only lasting kingdom is Christ's Kingdom! Hebrews 12:28 says, "Therefore let us be grateful for receiving a kingdom that cannot be shaken, and thus let us offer to God acceptable worship, with reverence and awe." Actually, I have learned that this world is not my home. The Apostle Paul declared in Philippians 3:20–21, "But our (believers') citizenship is in heaven, and from it we await a Savior, the Lord Jesus Christ, who will transform our lowly body to be like His glorious body, by the power that enables him even to subject all things to Himself." I am very thankful now to be a citizen of America, but I know that even America is not my lasting home.

The inspiration for the title of this book, and my life's story, comes from 1 Peter 1:1–9. Peter is writing to the elect exiles, scattered throughout the Roman Empire. They are elect and scattered according to the foreknowledge of God the Father, in the sanctification of the Spirit, for obedience to Jesus Christ and for sprinkling with His blood. According to God's mercy, He has caused them to be born again to a living hope through the resurrection of Jesus Christ from the dead, to *an inheritance that is imperishable, undefiled, and unfading, kept in heaven for them.* (Italics mine) Peter is addressing those that have no real home in this world, but have been granted, by God's great mercy, to receive new life (to be born again) to an

131

inheritance in heaven. This is *A Home to Call My Own!* My entire life story is evidence that God is true to His promise to Abraham, that God would bless the nations through his offspring (Genesis 12). God is so committed to redeem His people that He will not fail to bring to His Son the prize for which He died. The Father has given the Son authority to give eternal life to all whom the Father has given to the Son. That's right: all believers are a gift from the Father to the Son. Jesus' high priestly prayer in John 17:1–5 makes this point perfectly clear. John writes, "When Jesus had spoken these words, he lifted up his eyes to heaven, and said, "Father, the hour has come; glorify your Son that the Son may glorify you, since you have given him authority over all flesh, to give eternal life to all whom you have given him. And this is eternal life, that they know you the only true God, and Jesus Christ whom you have sent. I glorified you on earth, having accomplished the work that you gave me to do. And now, Father, glorify me in your own presence with the glory that I had with you before the world existed.

The Son of God sheds his blood for His people, redeems them, and keeps them for all eternity. No one can snatch them from his hand. He will raise them up on the last day! (John 6:39) Neither Adolph Hitler nor any other earthly ruler can stop our great God from redeeming his people, even if He has to drag them over the Atlantic Ocean to hear the Gospel and be saved! That is grace and grace alone is the story of all who trust in Christ!

Chapter 15

From Nyack to Today

Send the gospel of salvation to a world of dying men.
Tell it out to every nation till the Lord shall come again.
Go and tell them, go and tell them, Jesus died for sinful men.
Go and tell them, go and tell them, He is coming back again.
A.B. Simpson (1843–1919)

few things changed for me in 1959. I looked for
every opportunity to grow in my Christian experience by personal Bible study and attending church and our German
youth group. One opportunity was that the older German people
approached our young people to have German services for them.
This resulted in a city-wide campaign to reach German people. We
had ads in the *Cincinnati Enquirer* and on the radio station. Then
we made contact with a German pastor in Kitchener, Ontario, Pastor
Plaum, who consented to hold meetings. The result was that over
140 came the first day. Enough German people wanted a place of
their own. They organized a congregation, bought a house on Chase

Avenue, and converted it to a meeting place of their own. Within two years they outgrew the facility and bought six acres of land on Jessop Road, built a church there, and had as their preacher Sister Gertrud from Liberty Corner, who served them over ten years. Sister Gertrude was a strict disciplinarian, but sweet, knew her Scripture well, and was a good preacher. Everyone liked her. The church is still a full-fledged congregation to this day, but German is no longer the official language.

It was on a nice sunny Sunday morning in the early fall that I took one of our girls from our youth group after attending the German service downtown, back to her workplace in Hyde Park. She was usually off on weekends, but this Sunday she was asked to work. I knew that I could not make it back to downtown in time for the English service, so I stopped at a church in Hyde Park on Erie Avenue. Unknown to me then, it was a Christian and Missionary Alliance Church. The head usher welcomed me, and when he noticed my German accent, he gave me a German flag for my lapel. I was right at home in this place. They had what they called Missionary Convention for that week and had several missionary speakers. The church was packed. They had both a morning service and an evening service. Now that was new to me, going to church twice a day, but I enjoyed it. Great gospel singing and great preaching were going on there, not only during the convention but every Sunday. So I made it my church right away since they offered me what I was looking for, a Bible-teaching church that fit right in with my search for Bible growth and maturing. The Pastor's name was Rev. Liversedge, a very serious, mission-minded man. His life was dedicated for foreign missions and reaching the lost.

That whole week was an eye opener for me and my Lutheran background. The very thought of missions was new to me. I always thought that merely attending services was all that was required. I realized that the all believers have a greater purpose: to glorify God and proclaim the Gospel, the good news of Christ, around the world. Pastor Liversedge took me under his wing, so to speak. Every time we met he brought up missions. He thought every Christian should be on the foreign mission field! One day he asked me if I ever considered being involved in foreign missions. I told him no, but I said I would consider it if God had so called me.

One Sunday evening, after the service, I was invited by his wife and him to come over to his house with some other people I met that evening. After we ate some snacks, the conversation turned toward missions. Pastor Liversedge asked me again if I had considered my future as a foreign missionary. I told him I was open to the idea. (I was almost twenty-three years old now). He told me that he went to college in Nyack, New York, at the Nyack Missionary College. Rev. Liversedge kept asking me if I would go, and I finally said, "Yes!" He called the college, and they said I could still get in if I came up right away since registration was in two days. I quit my job and headed to Nyack a day later, on January 16, 1960. I received my acceptance papers two days later.

School was quite new to me, but I enjoyed it. I realized very quickly however that I was not prepared for it, either financially or spiritually. I had enough money for the first semester, but not for the next. I went back to Cincinnati in the summer of 1960 and stayed with my sister Gerda and her husband Jerry (Jurgen). I got various jobs that summer and made enough for the next semester, but that was all. I began to see God working in my life and answering prayer. Just one example was a prayer for a typewriter that I needed. All the papers in school had to be typewritten, but I did not have a typewriter. I was very discouraged, having only $5 to my name and no way to buy a typewriter. I went downtown to the Elgin Typewriter Company and looked for a used typewriter. They had one for $19, but I only had $5. I made a down payment with that $5 and told them I would come back in a week or two with the rest. On the way back, I stopped at Ault Park and told the Lord all my needs, including the typewriter. I went to prayer meeting on Wednesday night, and when I got home, there on the porch, sat a new typewriter, not the used one, and even a little stand to put the typewriter! To this day I have no idea who God used to bring this typewriter to me. The Lord supplied!

All together, I spent three years at Nyack. In my second year, the name changed from Nyack Missionary College simply to Nyack College. Also, the school became accredited and now had higher standards. Originally, when they accepted me, they did so based upon my German Trade School credits. Now I had to have an American high school diploma. That was a monkey wrench in my plans. I investigated my options and I enrolled in the Nyack High School evening preparatory classes to receive my high school diploma. After going also to night school, I finally took the test and passed, which was recognized by the State of New York. Proudly I went the registrar's office with my diploma only to be told that with their new accreditation, my program of study would be discontinued and I could not finish. Other foreign students had to endure the same decision from Nyack. I was very sad and disappointed with their decision, but finally accepted it is as a sign from the Lord. I stayed another year at Nyack in the hope they would provide another program of study for me, but nothing happened. In all I spent three years at Nyack College. They were good years, but I left because I would not be allowed to graduate. At first I was heartbroken over the whole situation, but with some counseling with some of the teachers I learned to accept it. The church I attended was also helpful in sorting out my life circumstances. I attended mostly the Tappan Alliance church in Tappan, New York. (As my sons read this part of my story, they felt compelled to write the president of Nyack College and explain this situation. Nyack College presented me with an honorary degree and my graduation celebration was held on June 6, 2014!)

It was a very small congregation of about twenty-five to thirty people, but it grew with time. Later, after I was married, we made it our family church. We got really involved with so many jobs there.

I taught Sunday school there, and Judith formed a choir and also played the organ. The church grew so that we had to build a bigger facility. In time, all three of our sons grew up there and as a family we really loved it. My time there was good, and we made many friends. The whole atmosphere was good. I supported my way by doing a lot of side jobs. My first job was with the college maintaining all their vehicles, making sure they all were serviced on time. I didn't have to do the job, but I took them to a service station when needed. They had four station wagons and a forty seat Blue Bird bus I later learned to drive. I drove the choral and the glee club to various churches and performances, receiving a whole $ 1.25 an hour. My paycheck for the month was usually $35. Also, since I had a car, I drove four girls who were nurses to the Suffern, New York hospital every Sunday. They usually gave me $1.25 each, and that was enough money for the week.

A few important things happened to me while on the Hillside which they called the College. I met my future wife there, Judith Wisser. I met her during the second semester that first year. She was a shy and quiet lady but somehow I set my affection on her. However, fellow students called her Mona Lisa because she was so identical to her. She was a PK (preacher's kid) and a little introverted, while I was just the opposite. Her father was an Alliance minister and pastored a church in Pittsburgh, Pennsylvania. On her birthday that year I tried to impress her with a bottle of a German perfume, 4711, a special treat. I had only $7.50 to my name and the bottle cost me $6.50, but I thought she was worth it. Well, she accepted my gift, but two days later she came to me and told me she would break it off with me and reflect a little of God's leading in her life. I was stunned, but in my own learning of God's leading in my life, I accepted it. Needless to say in a week's time she came back to me and asked if I would take her back, and our relationship grew. We were married on August 25, 1962. She also graduated from the college that same year with a degree in sacred music.

Judith and I had three sons: Timothy Mark, born February 5, 1964; Thomas Edward, born March 24, 1967; and William Robert, born February 28, 1971. In September of 1976, we moved to Cincinnati, Ohio. I purchased some land that my sister found. We left New Jersey behind and laid down roots in Loveland, Ohio, a suburb of Cincinnati. We lived between Loveland and Milford, but all three sons graduated from Milford High School. We lived on a private drive called Maranatha Way. I worked for the Fred B. DeBra Company. DeBra was a mechanical contractor that contracted with government facilities. My company later changed to Four Seasons, and it was with them I worked as a pipe fitter until my retirement in July of 2005.

We attended the Calvary Chapel Alliance Church once we moved to Cincinnati, and I'm still there to this day. I taught Sunday school, and Judith led the choir until her death. Judith passed from this life to be forever with her Lord on October 24, 2005. She had survived breast cancer and had been cancer-free for five years. Two weeks after major surgery, she developed a blood clot that went to her lung, taking her life in her sleep.

All three sons graduated from college, married wonderful ladies, and have families of their own. After high school (1982), Tim joined the Army National Guard and worked his way through Cedarville College (now Cedarville University) with a degree in business. Tim met his wife, Amy Phillips, at Cedarville, and they married on November 28, 1987. Their children are Jacob Timothy, born September 12, 1989; Joseph William, born August 8, 1991; and Annie Louise, born June 10, 1993. Tim and Amy presently live in Springfield, Ohio. Jacob graduated from Eastern Kentucky University in professional golf management and now lives in Cleveland, Ohio. Joey has finished three years of college and works and lives in Columbus, Ohio. Annie is completing her education at Campbellsville University in Kentucky. Annie plans to marry on July 26, 2014.

After high school (1985), Tom went to Ft. Wayne Bible College in Ft. Wayne, Indiana. The school changed its name in 1990, and Tom graduated from Summit Christian College with a degree in pastoral ministries. Tom met Patty Owens there, and they married on August 18, 1990. Their children are Benjamin Edward, born April 26, 1993 and Noah Thomas, born October 10, 1995. Ben has finished two years in college, learning graphic design, and Noah is finishing up high school. Tom, Patty, and their boys live in Manito, Illinois.

Bill headed south after high school (1989) and attended Toccoa Falls College in Toccoa, Georgia. He played soccer there for three seasons until an injury prevented him from playing his final year. Bill graduated from TFC in 1995 with a degree in pastoral ministries. While at college, Bill met his wife, Mary Beth Busbee, and they were married on June 20, 1992. They have two children, William Robert, Jr., born February 27, 1996 and Emmi Ruth (Emmi was named after my sister that died before I was born), born November 5, 1999. Will is a senior in high school, and Emmi is a high school freshman. Bill, Beth, and his children presently live in Blairsville, Georgia.

Looking back, I could never have planned my life like this! Only God, by His grace, could bless me like He has. I am thankful for my children and grandchildren, and not too long after Judith passed away, God sent me another gift. Her name is Audrey. I am thankful now to live my final days with this wonderful woman. We married on March 27, 2009.

My one and only desire is to know God more. I know I mentioned about a higher power working in my life at the beginning. That higher power is not an impersonal being. It is Yahweh, the Covenant God of Scripture. "God in three persons, blessed Trinity!" God the Father planned my life and redemption, God the Son purchased my redemption with His shed blood, and God the Holy Spirit applied the Gospel to my heart, removed the blinders, and caused me to see, "the light of the glory of God in the face of Jesus Christ" (2 Corinthians 4:6). By grace, this Triune God has given me life and has given me *A Home to Call My Own*. My prayer is that if I do not meet you in this life that I will meet you in the life to come. You also can have a home to call your own, if you call upon Christ today.

I will glory in my Redeemer, whose priceless blood has ransomed me.
Mine was the sin that drove the bitter nails and hung him on that judgment tree.
I will glory in my Redeemer who crushed the power of sin and death.
My only Savior before the Holy Judge.
The Lamb who is my righteousness.
The Lamb who is my righteousness.

I will glory in my Redeemer my life He bought my love He owns.
I have no longings for another, I'm satisfied in Him alone.
I will glory in my Redeemer, His faithfulness my standing place.
Though foes are mighty and rush upon me.
My feet are firm held by His grace.
My feet are firm held by His grace.

I will glory in my Redeemer who carries me on eagle's wings.
He crowns my life with loving-kindness,
His triumph song I'll ever song!
I will glory in my Redeemer who waits for me at gates of gold.
And when He calls me it will be paradise.
His face forever to behold!
His face forever to behold!

I Will Glory in My Redeemer
Words and music by Steve and Vicki Cook
Sovereign Grace Music

MY VISIT TO EAST PRUSSIA

*T*he end of June/July in 1999 my Sister Gerda and I went to East Prussia.

She had gone three years earlier and wanted me to experience the excitement of being there. Our plane went to Brussels, Oslo and finally arrived in Palanga, Lithuania. In Oslo, we boarded a small Russian commuter jet and took the almost two hour trip to Palanga. It was a modern little airport next to the Baltic Sea. We were greeted by Dr. Algis, a Lithuanian anestisiolgist, whom my sister met three years earlier, his wife, Vida, and an interpreter Elge. Later we also met their three year old daughter Urte. Dr Algis then took us to a fine restaurant before we got to Klaipeda (German name was Memel). It was only a 20 mile ride on a modern highway. Today, Klaipeda is a modern city, having been bombed to destruction during World War II. In one night more than 50,000 people died. The city has been rebuilt and one can see hardly a trace of the devastation.

I remember the city very well because my aunt Marta took us on vacation to go to the Kurische Nehrung, a strip of land between the mainland and the Baltic Sea. It was then a nice place with white sand and Dunes. It was a place where we kids ran all day. We also visited Schwarzord. I have many wonderful memories from my youth of that city, and the next city we traveled to, the city of Nidden, a fishing town.

Our luggage did not arrive with our plane, so we stayed close to Palanga that first day. On the second day arrived, we drove to my hometown of Stonischken, now called Stonishkai. As we entered our little village my heart just stopped. Fifty-five years before, when I left that little town as six year old, I could remember lots of streets and the beloved bahnhof, (the railroad station), where I was born. It was then a big building to me and now it looked rather small. Our small outhouse was still there and the well is still used to this day! So many sites in Stonischken were still the same. The bomb crater that hit 75 feet from our house was still there! We wanted to see our living quarters, but the family that lives there were very reluctant to let us in. Dr. Algis pleaded with her that we don't want to take her living quarters, but we only desired to see the place where lived before we fled. She reluctantly let us in. In it was every thing like we left it! The same color of paint and the old woodstove was just as I remembered it. We also wanted to see our living quarters, especially the room were I was born, but there was a big padlock hung on the door preventing us from entering. However, the stairwell was littered with empty beer bottles and pigeons all over. I think Squatters make their home there. We also found my mother's grave and the grave of my sister Emmi. We hunted through weeds six feet tall to find the graves, and only an old photograph was our guide.

.All around it was a sad day for me, but I rejoiced that day because it brought back so many memories. Then we went on another 3 kilometers to Plaschken where we went to church. The church was all bombed out and everything inside it was gone. The

Russians stored grain in it. The beautiful organ was also gone. The only thing left was bare walls. In Plaschken we met with some survivors who told us of some autracies that went on during the Russian occupation.

Then we went on another 2 kilometers to Pageldienen. My grandparent's house was removed for farm land. That was a common practice by the Russians at the time. Only the old schoolhouse was still standing. My sister went to school there. My observation was that Russia used East Prussia as their bread-basket and now everything was littered with their abandon equipment.

Then we went on to Rucken where I went to school. This is the place where I said my famous speech (my story in the book.) My classroom was still there, but the Russians enlarged the whole facility. We stayed overnight in a nice hotel in Shilute, formerly called Hydekruk, where my mother was in the hospital and subsequently died. Every thing was still there, but the hospital no longer had any records of my mother's time there.

It was now Sunday and we went to the only German church in Shilute. It was pastored by a German man who was once in a

Russian prison camp and was severely injured there. The next day we went to Raseinai where my mother went to see her girlfriend (Mrs.Lange in my book) every summer. From there it was only 8 km. to Shidlova, my mother's hometown. Here we found an old lady who also knew our family from years past and also my mother! She directed us to the old homestead, but the house was now gone. Grandpa's blacksmith shop was still there, but it was barely standing. The yard was full of currant berries and we helped ourselves to a good lunch. There was an old woman next door who also remembered a little about my mother, but after she married she lost all contact with her. The building my mother's brother had for a saw mill was still standing. He came to America after WWI and I lived with them in Cincinnati for 2 ½ years. It was good to see all these towns and villages, and the wonderful heritage I had. It was good to me to see all my childhood places and relive some memories.

The rest of my trip was spent in Lithuania proper. The memory that stuck out and impressed my mind the most was the hills full of crosses, literally millions of them. The Lithuanians placed these crosses for loved ones lost in the war as a memorial. There are many stories about this whole hill, some even miraculous. The Russians tried to get rid of these, but to no avail. Once the Russians bulldozed them but the next day they were there again. They tried to build a reservoir there and crosses again sprang up the next day. God had done marvelous things in Lithuania.

The day came when we said good bye to Dr.Algis and his wife, Vida. We left for Berlin to see my ailing Tante Martha who courageously saw me and my sister come through all the war years.

Auf wiedersehn Memelland

CPSIA information can be obtained
at www.ICGtesting.com
Printed in the USA
LVOW05s1927030817
543647LV00028B/1439/P